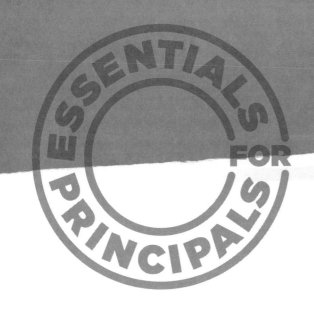

The School Leader's Guide to
English Learners

D1405354

DOUGLAS FISHER
NANCY FREY

A Joint Publication

Solution Tree naesp™

555 North Morton Street
Bloomington, IN 47404
800.733.6786 (toll free) / 812.336.7700
FAX: 812.336.7790

email: info@solution-tree.com
solution-tree.com

Printed in the United States of America

15 14 13 12 11   1 2 3 4 5

Library of Congress Cataloging-in-Publication Data

Fisher, Douglas, 1965-

    Essentials for principals : the school leader's guide to English learners / Douglas Fisher, Nancy Frey.

        p. cm.

    Includes index.

    ISBN 978-1-936765-17-1 (perfect bound) -- ISBN 978-1-936765-18-8 (library edition) 1. English language--Study and teaching--Foreign speakers. I. Frey, Nancy, 1959- II. Title.

    PE1128.A2F547 2012

    425.0071'073--dc23

                                        2011048416

Solution Tree
Jeffrey C. Jones, CEO
Edmund M. Ackerman, President

Solution Tree Press
President: Douglas M. Rife
Publisher: Robert D. Clouse
Vice President of Production: Gretchen Knapp
Managing Production Editor: Caroline Wise
Senior Production Editor: Edward M. Levy
Proofreader: Rachel Rosolina
Text and Cover Designer: Jenn Taylor

ACKNOWLEDGMENTS

Solution Tree Press would like to thank the following reviewers:

Carla L. Claycomb
Director of Educational Services Division
Pennsylvania State Education Association
Harrisburg, Pennsylvania

Ester Johanna De Jong
Associate Professor, Department of Teaching
  and Learning
University of Florida
Gainesville, Florida

Margo DelliCarpini
Editor, *TESOL Journal*
Associate Professor and Chair, Department of
  Middle and High School Education
Lehman College, City University of New York
New York, New York

Leroy Gaines
Principal
Acorn Woodland Elementary School
Oakland, California

Claude Goldenberg
Professor, School of Education
Stanford University
Stanford, California

Elena Izquierdo
Associate Professor, Teacher Education
University of Texas at El Paso
El Paso, Texas

Liliana Minaya-Rowe
Professor Emerita, Neag School of Education
University of Connecticut
Storrs, Connecticut

Edward J. Schumacher
Principal
Russell Boulevard Elementary
Columbia, Missouri

Kathryn Sperling
English Language Development Teacher
Concord International Elementary School
Seattle, Washington

Denise Stewart
English Language Development Coordinator
San José Unified School District
San José, California

Martha Tinnin
Third-Grade Dual Language Teacher
Cox Elementary School
Wylie, Texas

Visit **go.solution-tree.com/ELL**
to download the reproducibles in this book.

TABLE OF CONTENTS

Reproducible pages are in italics.

ABOUT THE AUTHORS

Douglas Fisher, PhD, is professor of educational leadership at San Diego State University and a teacher leader at Health Sciences High and Middle College in San Diego, California. He teaches courses in instructional improvement, differentiated instruction, policy, research, and literacy. As a teacher, he focuses on English language arts instruction across the grade levels. He was the codirector for the Center for the Advancement of Reading and has served as coach for the Chula Vista Elementary School District in Chula Vista, California. He was formerly director of professional development for the City Heights Educational Collaborative and also taught English at Hoover High School, both in San Diego.

Douglas has written numerous articles on reading and literacy, differentiated instruction, and curriculum design. His books include *Creating Literacy-Rich Schools for Adolescents*, *Checking for Understanding*, *Better Learning Through Structured Teaching*, and *Content-Area Conversations*.

He received an International Reading Association Celebrate Literacy Award for his work on literacy leadership. For his work as codirector of the City Heights Professional Development Schools, he received the Christa McAuliffe award. He was also corecipient of the Farmer Award for excellence in writing from the National Council of Teachers of English for the article "Using Graphic Novels, Anime, and the Internet in an Urban High School," published in the *English Journal*.

Douglas earned a bachelor's degree in communication, a master's degree in public health, and a doctoral degree in multicultural education, all from San Diego State University, and an executive master's degree in business from Claremont Graduate University. He has also completed postdoctoral study at the National Association of State Boards of Education focused on standards-based reforms.

Nancy Frey, PhD, is a professor of literacy in the School of Teacher Education at San Diego State University. Through the university's teacher-credentialing and reading-specialist programs, she teaches courses on elementary and secondary reading instruction and literacy in content areas, classroom management, and supporting students with diverse learning needs. Nancy also teaches classes at Health Sciences High and Middle College in San Diego. She is a board member of the California Reading Association and a credentialed special educator and reading specialist in California. She was previously a public school teacher in Florida, working for the Florida Inclusion Network to help districts design systems for supporting students with disabilities in general education classrooms.

Nancy is the recipient of the 2008 Early Career Achievement Award from the National Reading Conference and the Christa McAuliffe Award for excellence in teacher education from the American Association of State Colleges and Universities. With Douglas Fisher, she was corecipient of the Farmer Award for excellence in writing from the National Council of Teachers of English.

She is coauthor of *Checking for Understanding, Better Learning Through Structured Teaching,*, and *Content-Area Conversations*. She has written articles for *The Reading Teacher, Journal of Adolescent and Adult Literacy, English Journal, Voices in the Middle, Middle School Journal, Remedial and Special Education,* and *Educational Leadership*.

Nancy received a bachelor's degree from Florida Atlantic University, a master's degree focusing on curriculum and instruction from San Diego State University, and a PhD in education, with an emphasis on reading and language arts, from Claremont Graduate School and San Diego State University.

Visit www.fisherandfrey.com to learn more about Douglas's and Nancy's work.

To book Douglas or Nancy for professional development, contact pd@solution-tree.com.

INTRODUCTION

The English learner population is rapidly increasing throughout the United States. English learner enrollment grew by 51 percent between 1999 and 2009, while K–12 enrollment remained relatively stable, growing a mere 10 percent (National Clearinghouse for English Language Acquisition, 2011). During that same period, fourteen individual states from Oregon to Kansas to the Carolinas saw growth rates for English learners of over 200 percent.

Data from the census provide a vivid picture of the changing demographics of the United States. Six states—California, Texas, New York, Florida, Illinois, and New Jersey—account for a large majority of children of immigrants (69 percent of the nation's total). Although these states appear to be the first stop for many immigrants, other states have exceedingly rapid rates of immigration: 206 percent growth in Nevada, 153 percent in North Carolina, 148 percent in Georgia, and 125 percent in Nebraska (Capps et al., 2005).

Perhaps your interest in the education of English learners stems from the lack of achievement many of them experience. While current federal legislation focuses attention on outcomes, principals want to know how to meet the increasingly high expectations being set for these students. Thankfully, there is evidence for what works and what doesn't, in terms of reaching high levels of success. While there are still areas of disagreement in terms of the education of English learners, a principal can take concrete actions to ensure that the school rallies resources to meet their needs.

The interest of some of you in this topic may be more localized. Perhaps you've just met a new student and his or her family. You might have struggled to communicate with this student and found yourself frustrated when you tried to explain the educational system to the parents. Your interest might have been spurred because you know that families are key to the success of children.

We have organized this book around the following five big ideas that we think principals concerned about English learners should know:

1. English learners are a diverse group with individual needs that can be addressed by understanding proficiency levels and holding reasonable expectations.

2. English learners are doubly challenged, as they must learn English while learning *in* English. They benefit from quality instructional programs that emphasize student talk, in order to give them lots of experiences using academic language.

3. Assessment for English learners requires attention to the whole child. This multidimensional approach is necessary in order for a true picture to emerge. It requires balancing large-scale assessments with individualized informal ones that highlight strengths and do not simply catalog deficits.

4. Response to instruction and intervention (RTI^2) with English learners is complex because of the many factors that influence second language development. English learners deserve supplemental and intensive interventions, especially when their performance pales in comparison with true peers, not just chronological ones.

5. A quality program for English learners is developed and improved only with the participation of stakeholders. These include educators and personnel at the school, students and their families, and middle schools that your students will attend in the future. There is much to be learned from these stakeholders as research continues to shape policy and practice.

In the chapters that follow, we explore each of these big ideas and provide practical information about how to implement them in real schools.

Learning About English Learners

Juan Rodriguez has just moved into your area and wants to enroll his son Antonio in your middle school. Of course, you're excited to meet this new student, and you recognize the trust this family has placed in your hands. You know it is an honor to provide educational services for students and to watch them grow into contributing members of society. You thank the parents for their confidence in your school and remind them of dismissal times and the after-school programs offered on your campus. Understanding that every new student is a bit uncomfortable with a new school, you walk Antonio to his classroom and introduce him to a gregarious peer, Eric.

Big Idea

English learners are a diverse group with individual needs that can be addressed by understanding proficiency levels and holding reasonable expectations.

Questions Principals Ask

- What tools are used to determine if a student is an English learner?
- What are the different types or classifications of English learners?
- How does English proficiency change?
- What are the language standards for English learners?

During this first week of school, Antonio will participate in a number of assessments, including several screening tools, to determine his instructional needs and any gaps in his knowledge. In thinking about which screening tools to use, you remember that the responses to the home language survey indicated that Antonio speaks Spanish at home. The home language survey is a common starting place for determining if a student is an English learner.

Home Language Survey

In nearly every state in the United States, the identification of English learners begins with a survey given to parents that solicits information about the languages their child uses. The home language survey is so common that many people believe it is required under federal law. In fact, there is no U.S. law that mandates the home language survey. Rather, the law requires states to identify students who need language support in order to be successful in school. Unfortunately, these students are currently labeled with the derogatory term *limited English proficient* (LEP). We prefer the term *English learner*, a more contemporary designation for students who are adding English to their literacy skills. Federal law also defines a student in need of language support as one "who comes from an environment where a language other than English has had a significant impact on the individual's level of English language proficiency" or who "comes from an environment where a language other than English is dominant" (No Child Left Behind Act, 2008).

Research on the use of the home language survey as a valuable tool is inconclusive. Some studies report positive relationships between the home language survey and instructional needs and outcomes (for example, Townsend & Collins, 2008), and others report weak or nonexistent relationships (for example, Abedi, Lord, & Plummer, 1997). Until there is a better tool, the home language survey will likely be used to identify students who need additional assessment. Alison Bailey and Kimberly Kelly (2010) provide an overview of home language survey questions from several states, and figure 1.1 shows a sample home language survey containing the four most common languages in our community, San Diego—English, Spanish, Somali, and Tagalog.

As Alex Ragan and Nonie Lesaux (2006) have noted, states can recommend a number of different actions based on the findings of the home language survey. In some states, the survey is followed by a test of English language proficiency. In others, the policy requires "additional criteria including parental request or approval, teacher input, student achievement, and the recommendations of an LEP committee or similarly named group of educators who convene to monitor ELLs' progress" (p. 14). It is important to understand state and district policies so that your school remains in compliance. In addition, be aware that services and programs for English learners are monitored regularly. These compliance visits are used to ensure that students' rights are upheld and that the school is in compliance with federal laws, including the Civil Rights Act of 1964, which is the basis for the laws, lawsuits, and regulations we will discuss further in chapter 2 (page 15).

Our new student, Antonio, took the California English Language Development Test (CELDT), the proficiency test used in that state. As is the case in several other states (including Arizona, Colorado, Florida, Illinois, and Texas), children who are in kindergarten and first grade in California are assessed on listening and speaking, and students in grade 2 and beyond are also assessed for reading and writing skills. In other states (including, New Jersey, Georgia, New Mexico, and New York), there are no differences between what is assessed at different grade levels; the same tools are used in kindergarten through grade 12. Based on his CELDT score indicating that he is not yet fluent in English, Antonio is classified as an English learner. According to the law, he has "limited English proficiency" and requires instructional support to be successful.

In addition to the assessment of English proficiency, many states require that students identified as English learners be assessed in their primary language if at all possible. Primary language assessments are available in some languages. Importantly, staff members who are fluent in the language should administer and score the primary language assessment, if it is going to be useful. Antonio took the Spanish Idea Proficiency Test, published by Ballard and Tighe, which indicated that he has nearly grade-level proficiency in his home language. If no primary language survey is

Home Language Assessment Survey

Date	School
Fecha	Escuela
Petsa	Paaralan
Taariikh	Dugsi

Please answer the following questions:
Favor de contestar las siguientes preguntas:
Pakisagot ang mga sumusunod na tanong:
Fadlan waxaad kajawaabtaa su'aalahan soo socda:

1. Name of student	Last	First	Middle	Grade	Birth date
Nombre del alumno	Apellido	Primero	Segundo	Grado	Fecha de Nacimiento
Pangalan ng mag-aaral	Apelyido	Una	Apelyido ng Ina	Baytang	Kapanganakan
Magaca ardeyga	Magaca Awoowga	Magacaaga	Magaca Aabbaha	Heerka Fasalka	Taariikhda Dhalashada

2. Which language did your son or daughter learn when he or she first began to talk?
¿Cuándo su hijo o hija empezó a hablar- ¿cuál idioma aprendió primero?
Aling wika ang natutunan ng iyong anak noong siya ay nagsimulang magsalita?
Luuqadee ayuu ilmahaagu ku af-bartay?

3. What language does your son or daughter most frequently use with adults in the home?
¿Cuál idioma usa principalmente su hijo o hija cuando conversa con adultos de su casa?
Anong wika ang pinakamalimit gamitin ng iyong anak sa mga nakatatandang kasama sa tahanan?
Dadka waaweyn ee guriga jooga, luuqadee ayuu ilmahaagu kula hadlaa inta badan?

4. Which language is used most frequently by the adults in your home?
¿Cuál idioma usan los adultos de su casa con más frecuencia cuando conversan entre ellos mismos?
Aling wika ang pinaka-malimit gamitin ng mga nakatatanda sa inyong tahanan?
Dadka waaweyn ee guriga joogi, luuqadee ayay ku hadlaan inta badan?

5. What language do you use most frequently to speak to your son or daughter?
¿Cuál idioma usa Ud. con más frecuencia cuando habla con su hijo o hija?
Anong wika ang pinakamalimit mong gamitin sa pakikipag-usap sa iyong anak?
Ilmahaaga, luuqadee ayaad kula hadashaa inta badan?

Signature of parent or guardian
Firma del padre de familia o tutor
Lagda ng magulang o tagapangalaga
Saxiixa waalidka ama qotka ilmaha masuulka ka ah

This information will be used by the district and the Office for Civil Rights of the U.S. Department of Education to develop school programs.
Esta información se usará por el distrito escolar y La Oficina de Derechos Civiles para desarrollar program as escolares.
Ang impormasyong ito ay gagamitin ng Tanggapan ng Karapatang Sibil ng Distrito at ng U.S. sa pagbalangkas ng mga programang pampaaralan
Degmadu iyo xafiiska Xuquuqda Madanigu waxay u isticmaali doonaan warbixintan si ay u horumariyaan xirfadaha dugsiyada waxbarashada.

Figure 1.1: A language assessment survey in four languages.

available, school systems often use an informal inventory, like the reproducible Primary Language Informal Assessment (page 14 and online at **go.solution-tree.com/ELL**).

Amal Abdi enrolled in school on the same day as Antonio. She was also greeted by the principal, walked to class, and introduced to several other students. In their responses to the home language survey, her parents answered "English" to all the questions. Based on this information alone, Amal is not identified as an English learner, and her classification is "English only." This does not mean that she is monolingual. In fact, Amal also speaks Harari and Amharic, since she lived in Ethiopia. This is an example of how the home language survey, while useful, can miss information about students. While the survey is an important and quick screening tool in the identification of English learners, there need to be opportunities to provide English learner support based on teacher recommendation and student performance.

Classifications of English Learners

Based on the home language survey and subsequent information obtained about the student and his or her language, schools can make general classifications. However, it is important to note that these broad categories provide little information about the instructional needs of individual students. Within any one of them, students will have a range of differences, strengths, and needs. We present them here because they are used to discuss trends, and you are likely to hear these terms. A longer glossary, including these terms, can be found on page 69.

- **English only:** In most cases, this classification will apply to students who are monolingual English speakers, but it is important to remember that this is not always the case. Amal was classified this way based on her home language survey.

- **English learner (EL):** In most cases, this classification means LEP. We will discuss various proficiency levels for English learners in the next section of this chapter. In chapter 2 (page 15), we will discuss the diversity of English learners, who are the focus of this book, and the various program models used to educate them.

- **Initially fluent English proficient (IFEP):** When the home language survey indicates languages other than English and the student scores proficient on the English proficiency test, the student is classified as fluent. This means that the student speaks languages in addition to English and that there is initial evidence that the student has proficiency in English. This is probably the better classification for Amal, but since her English proficiency was not assessed, she cannot be classified as IFEP. In fact, at this time, the school system has no information about her English proficiency.

- **Redesignated fluent English proficient (RFEP):** This classification is used for students who have been previously identified as English learners and have met some exit criteria. In most states, the exit criteria include a formal measure of English proficiency. Depending on the state, there may be additional criteria such as parent request or notification, teacher evaluation, review of an LEP committee, and academic performance in content areas other than English (Ragan & Lesaux, 2006). In many states, there are specific guidelines for monitoring student success after reclassification from English learner. Additional information about follow-up monitoring can be found in chapter 4 (page 43). As an example, Eric, the gregarious peer Antonio was introduced to on his first day, was redesignated that school year. At home, he spoke Vietnamese and some English, according to the home language survey. His English proficiency on the CELDT was intermediate, or developing. After a couple of years of school, Eric's proficiency increased to advanced, or bridging; he scored well on the state standards test, and his teacher and parents recommended redesignation. His classroom is now a mainstream English cluster, which provides support for English learners through specially designed academic instruction. This will also be explored further in chapter 2.

- **Newcomer:** While not a classification system used in databases, the term *newcomer* is often used to describe students who are new to English. Unfortunately, this designation is overused. Newcomers, by definition, are recent arrivals to the United States who have limited formal schooling and perform significantly below grade level. Traditionally, the designation of newcomer is reserved for students in grades 3 and higher, since younger students are not often missing years of schooling, due in part to the fact that they were only recently eligible to attend. The identification of a newcomer involves additional screening questions, such as:

  › Has the student been out of school for the last year or more?

  › Has the student completed less than three years of schooling?

  › Is the student lacking beginning literacy skills in his or her primary language?

  › Is the student in need of beginning orientation to school organization and culture?

Yes answers to questions like these indicate a student is at even greater risk compared with other English learners. In response, districts with significant numbers of newcomers often establish classes and special programs to socialize them into formal school and provide basic English language development (Short & Boyson, 2004).

Principals need to ensure that teachers have accurate information about students' English learner status and classification. While this information is not sufficient for instructional planning, it does provide teachers with information about students' language experiences, alerts them to students' needs, and reminds them to look for students' proficiency levels so they can plan appropriate instruction. It also alerts teachers to monitor students who have been redesignated.

Proficiency Levels of English Learners

As we have suggested, English learners progress through stages as they reach increasing proficiency. Typically, proficiency starts with a silent phase in which the student does very little talking. We've all seen a student who seems shy but is taking in everything. In all likelihood, if this shy student is an English learner, he or she is assimilating the sounds of English and learning basic vocabulary. We're reminded of Sari, a wide-eyed and inquisitive student who emigrated from Cambodia. With support and a risk-free environment, Sari started talking in no time, on her way to academic success and English proficiency. However, the respectful treatment of her silent period, which gave her the time to become more comfortable with her early attempts, was critical for her language development.

As students like Sari develop language, they move through a continuum of increasing skill and understanding. The membership organization Teachers of English to Speakers of Other Languages (TESOL, www.tesol.org), in collaboration with World-Class Instructional Design and Assessment (WIDA, www.wida.us), has identified five proficiency levels: entering, beginning, developing, expanding, and bridging (TESOL, 2006). Most states have developed sets of standards for these proficiency levels, though they may call them by other names. In California, they are *beginning, early intermediate, intermediate, early advanced,* and *advanced*; other states use levels 1, 2, 3, 4, and 5. The descriptors in table 1.1 encompass four interrelated components of communication: social and academic language functions, vocabulary (word level), grammar (sentence level), and discourse (extended text level).

To paint a more detailed picture, table 1.1 shows descriptors of the skills and behaviors common for students at different levels of proficiency (Rothenberg & Fisher, 2007). Most states list the five categories shown in the table, determined by formal assessments, but the descriptors vary state to state, so we have chosen to highlight the major differences using three broad categories—beginning, intermediate, and advanced (table 1.2).

Table 1.1: Performance Definitions for Five Levels of English Language Proficiency

Level 1 Starting	Level 2 Emerging	Level 3 Developing	Level 4 Expanding	Level 5 Bridging
English language learners can understand and use . . .				
. . . language to communicate with others around basic concrete needs.	. . . language to draw on simple and routine experiences to communicate with others.	. . . language to communicate with others on familiar matters regularly encountered.	. . . language in both concrete and abstract situations and apply language to new experiences.	. . . a wide range of longer oral and written texts and recognize implicit meaning.
. . . high-frequency words and memorized chunks of language.	. . . high-frequency and some general academic vocabulary and expressions.	. . . general and some specialized academic vocabulary and expressions.	. . . specialized and some technical academic vocabulary and expressions.	. . . technical academic vocabulary and expressions.
. . . words, phrases, or chunks of language.	. . . phrases or short sentences in oral or written communication.	. . . expanded sentences in oral or written communication.	. . . a variety of sentence lengths of varying linguistic complexity in oral and written communication.	. . . a variety of sentence lengths of varying linguistic complexity in extended oral or written discourse.
. . . pictorial, graphic, or nonverbal representation language.	. . . oral or written language, making errors that often impede the meaning of the communication.	. . . oral or written language, making errors that may impede the communication but retain much of its meaning.	. . . oral or written language, making minimal errors that do not impede the overall meaning of the communication.	. . . oral or written language approaching comparability to that of English-proficient peers.

Source: PreK–12 English Language Proficiency Standards: Augmentation of the World-Class Instructional Design and Assessment (WIDA) Consortium English Language Proficiency Standards. © 2006, *Teachers of English to Speakers of Other Languages (TESOL), Alexandria, VA: Reproduced with permission.*

Table 1.2: Skills and Behaviors at Three Proficiency Levels

	Beginner	Intermediate	Advanced
Listening and Speaking	• Answer simple questions with one- or two-word responses. • Respond to simple directions and questions by using physical actions and other means of nonverbal communication (for example, matching objects, pointing to an answer, drawing pictures). • Begin to speak with a few words or sentences by using a few standard English grammatical forms and sounds (for example, single words or phrases). • Use common social greetings and simple repetitive phrases independently (for example, "Thank you" and "You're welcome"). • Ask and answer questions by using phrases or simple sentences. • Retell stories by using appropriate gestures, expressions, and illustrative objects.	• Ask and answer instructional questions by using simple sentences. • Listen attentively to stories and information and identify important details and concepts by using both verbal and nonverbal responses. • Ask and answer instructional questions with some supporting elements (for example, "Which part of the story was the most important?"). • Participate in social conversations with peers and adults on familiar topics by asking and answering questions and soliciting information. • Make oneself understood when speaking by using consistent standard English grammatical forms and sounds; however, some rules are not followed (for example, third-person singular, male and female pronouns).	• Demonstrate understanding of most idiomatic expressions (for example, "Give me a hand") by responding to such expressions and using them appropriately. • Negotiate and initiate social conversations by questioning, restating, soliciting information, and paraphrasing the communication of others.
Reading	• Recognize and produce the English phonemes that are like the phonemes students hear and produce in their primary language. • Recognize and produce English phonemes that are unlike the phonemes students hear and produce in their primary language. • Produce most English phonemes while beginning to read aloud. • Produce simple vocabulary, such as single words or very short phrases, to communicate basic needs in social and academic settings (for example, locations, greetings, classroom objects). • Demonstrate comprehension of simple vocabulary with an appropriate action. • Retell stories by using simple words, phrases, and sentences.	• Produce English phonemes while reading aloud. • Recognize sound and symbol relationships and basic word-formation rules in written text (for example, basic syllabication rules and phonics). • Apply knowledge of English phonemes in oral and silent reading to derive meaning from literature and texts in content areas. • Use more complex vocabulary and sentences to communicate needs and express ideas in a wider variety of social and academic settings. • Recognize simple antonyms and synonyms (*good* and *bad*, *blend* and *mix*) in written text. Expand recognition of them, and begin to use them appropriately.	• Apply knowledge of sound and symbol relationships and basic word-formation rules to derive meaning from written text (for example, basic syllabication rules, regular and irregular plurals, and basic phonics). • Apply knowledge of academic and social vocabulary while reading independently. • Be able to use a standard dictionary to find the meanings of unfamiliar words. • Interpret the meaning of unknown words by using knowledge gained from previously read text. • Understand idioms, analogies, and metaphors in conversation and written text.

continued →

Reading		
• Recognize simple affixes (*educate*, *education*), prefixes (*dislike*, *preheat*), synonyms (*big*, *large*), and antonyms (*hot*, *cold*).	• Apply knowledge of vocabulary to discussions related to reading tasks.	• Read and orally respond to familiar stories and other texts by answering factual comprehension questions about cause-and-effect relationships.
• Begin to use knowledge of simple affixes, prefixes, synonyms, and antonyms to interpret the meaning of unknown words.	• Read simple vocabulary, phrases, and sentences independently.	• Read and orally respond to stories and texts from content areas by restating facts and details to clarify ideas.
• Recognize the difference between the use of the first- and third-person points of view in phrases or simple sentences.	• Read narrative and expository texts aloud with the correct pacing, intonation, and expression.	• Explain how understanding of text is affected by patterns of organization, repetition of main ideas, syntax, and word choice.
• Respond orally to stories read aloud and use physical actions and other means of nonverbal communication (for example, matching objects, pointing to an answer, drawing pictures).	• Use expanded vocabulary and descriptive words in oral and written responses to written texts.	• Write a brief summary (two or three paragraphs) of a story.
• Respond orally to stories read aloud, giving one- to two-word responses in answer to factual comprehension questions (who, what, when, where, and how).	• Recognize and understand simple idioms, analogies, and figures of speech in written text.	
	• Recognize that some words have multiple meanings and apply this knowledge to written text.	
	• Recognize the function of connectors in written text (for example, *first, then, after that, finally*).	
	• Understand and follow simple written directions for classroom-related activities.	
	• Read text, orally identify the main ideas, and draw inferences about the text by using detailed sentences.	
	• Read and identify basic text features, such as the title, table of contents, and chapter headings.	
	• Respond to comprehension questions about text by using detailed sentences (for example, "The brown bear lives with his family in the forest").	
Writing		
• Copy the alphabet legibly.	• Write legible, simple sentences that respond to topics in language arts and other content areas (for example, math, science, history, and social science).	• Develop a clear thesis and support it by using analogies, quotations, and facts appropriately.
• Copy words posted and commonly used in the classroom in labels, number names, days of the week, and months, for example.	• Follow a model given by the teacher to independently write a short paragraph of at least four sentences.	• Write a multiparagraph essay with consistent use of standard grammatical forms.
• Write simple sentences by using key words commonly used in the classroom in labels, number names, days of the week, and months, for example.		

	Beginner	Intermediate	Advanced
Writing	• Write phrases and simple sentences that follow English syntactical order.	• Create cohesive paragraphs that develop a central idea and consistently use standard English grammatical forms, even though some rules may not be followed. • Write simple sentences about an event or a character from a written text. • Produce independent writing that is understood when read but may include inconsistent use of standard grammatical forms.	

Language Standards for English Learners

TESOL (2006) has developed a set of preK–12 English language proficiency standards that can guide instruction across the content areas. These five standards cross the four domains of language—listening, speaking, reading, and writing—and address the dual goals for our English learners—proficiency in English and achievement in the core content areas. While content standards still drive curriculum, these TESOL standards guide instructional planning for English learners:

> Standard 1: English language learners **communicate** for **social, intercultural,** and **instructional** purposes within the school setting.
>
> Standard 2: English language learners **communicate** information, ideas, and concepts necessary for academic success in the area of **language arts.**
>
> Standard 3: English language learners **communicate** information, ideas, and concepts necessary for academic success in the area of **mathematics.**
>
> Standard 4: English language learners **communicate** information, ideas, and concepts necessary for academic success in the area of **science.**
>
> Standard 5: English language learners **communicate** information, ideas, and concepts necessary for academic success in the area of **social studies.** (p. 28)

These standards remind us that the ability to communicate permeates everything we do, in the classroom and beyond its walls. Thus, teachers must ensure that they have addressed the linguistic, not just the academic, demands of the content or task. In other words, every lesson has to be analyzed for the linguistic opportunities provided for students. Teachers, especially those who were not English learners when they were in school, need to be reminded that English learners are doing double the work: they are tasked with learning content and language simultaneously (Short & Fitzsimmons, 2007).

One way to ensure that appropriate support is provided to English learners is to encourage teachers to have a language objective for each of their content objectives (Echevarria, Vogt, &

Short, 2010). In our study of over three hundred teachers, we identified three types of language objectives (Fisher & Frey, 2010b):

1. **Vocabulary**—Probably the most common type of language objective is based on the vocabulary that students need to know. When teachers analyze their lessons, they may notice that there are specialized words—words with multiple meanings—that need attention. For example, a lesson on the human body includes words such as *tissue*, *vessel*, and *feet* that have multiple meanings. Alternatively, when teachers analyze their lessons, they will notice that there are technical words—words specific to the discipline—that need attention. For example, the lesson on the human body also includes *trachea*, *alveoli*, and *esophagus*. The language objective could focus on either specialized or technical words, though probably on different days.

2. **Structure**—The English language has a structure that students must come to understand. Accordingly, teachers can establish a language objective designed to ensure that students learn grammar and syntax. For example, teachers might focus on subject and verb agreement in students' talk or ask them to use signal words, such as *first*, *next*, *then*, and *finally*, in their writing. By attending to the structure of the language, English learners begin to generalize their understanding of the language conventions.

3. **Function**—Language is used for a purpose, whether it be to inform, entertain, persuade, or for any of a host of other reasons. Helping students match their speaking and writing with a specific function requires sophisticated thinking and planning. When students understand the expected language function, they are tasked with remaining true to that function and developing their ideas.

Table 1.3 contains a number of examples of language purpose statements from various content areas. Although it is beyond the scope of this book, many other resources exist for teachers who want to provide students with this type of support. Our purpose here is to remind principals that achievement rises when students know what to pay attention to. This is consistent with the findings of Jana Echevarria, Deborah Short, and Kristin Powers (2006); in their seven-year study, they found that analysis of the language demand of the task, paired with stated purposes about written and verbal language production, resulted in higher levels of achievement for English learners. As Jane Hill and Kathleen Flynn (2006, p. 22) note, "The educational environment also becomes a friendlier place for ELLs when they have a clearly stated target for learning."

Conclusion

Determining which students are English learners and which are not is an important task required of the principal. Although there will be support from the district office and guidance from state regulations, compliance often falls to the site administrator. For example, it is up to the principal to ensure that the home language survey is administered to each new student who enrolls. It's also up to the principal to ensure that the additional strategies for determining English learner status are implemented.

Table 1.3: Language Purpose Statements From Four Content Areas

Content Area	Vocabulary	Structure	Function
Mathematics	Highlight addition signal words in a word problem.	Use *less than*, *equal to*, or *greater than* to compare groups or numbers.	Describe the relationship between numbers in expanded form and standard form.
Social Studies	Name the routes and explorers on a map.	Sequence the steps of food production using the signal words *first*, *then*, *next*, and *finally*.	Justify in a paragraph the ways fire was used for hunting, cooking, and warmth by citing three examples.
Language Arts	Use *who*, *what*, and *why* to ask a question of your partner.	Identify the verb tenses used in the reading to explain what happened long ago and what will happen in the future.	Explain what organizational pattern was used by the writer, and critique its adequacy.
Science	Label a diagram of the digestive system (teeth, mouth, esophagus, stomach, small intestine, large intestine, colon).	Use the sentence frame "Some spiders _____, but other spiders_____."	Be able to tell my team members three ways that an environment can change.

Source: Unpacking the Language Purpose: Vocabulary, Structure, and Function, *by Douglas Fisher and Nancy Frey.* © 2010, *Teachers of English to Speakers of Other Languages (TESOL), Alexandria, VA: Reprinted with permission.*

It's also important for a principal to understand the language used in professional discussions about English learners, including categorical identification and language proficiency; teachers look to the principal for leadership and guidance in meeting students' needs. One specific support for English learners that the principal can provide is the use of language objectives. This may involve professional development, feedback, and setting out clear expectations. The effort is worth it. Students like Antonio need to learn language to participate in the world around them.

Primary Language Informal Assessment

Date: _____ Interviewer: _____

Information provided by (check one):

☐ Student

☐ Parent

☐ Other _____

Student name: _____ ID Number: _____

School: _____ Grade: _____

Language(s) other than English identified on the home language survey: _____

1. How many years of school has the student attended? _____

2. Where was the school located? _____

3. What is highest grade level the student reached? _____

4. What language(s) does the student use with friends, brothers and sisters, grandparents, extended family, and/or neighbors? _____

5. Can the student read in _____?   ☐ yes   ☐ no

6. Can the student write in _____?   ☐ yes   ☐ no

7. Is the student being taught _____ privately?   ☐ yes   ☐ no

8. Is the student's language the same, worse, or better than peers who are the same age?

CHAPTER 2

Developing a Quality Program for English Learners

The students who arrive at our schools bring with them a host of experiences, learning profiles, and family supports. English learners aren't uniformly the same, even when they share a heritage language, any more than monolingual English students are. Some students enter the kindergarten classroom with years of preschool education. For others, this may be their first contact with a school, regardless of chronological age. Students with extensive development in their first language are likely to use it to leverage learning a second, while those who have limited vocabulary will take longer to reach proficiency in English. In all cases, English learners have unique family and life experiences that influence their learning. This presents a host of challenges for schools as they attempt to tailor curricular, instructional, and programmatic approaches to better serve individual students.

Big Idea

English learners are doubly chalenged, as they must learn English while learning *in* English. They benefit from quality instructional programs that emphasize student talk in order to give them lots of experiences using academic language.

Questions Principals Ask

- What variables make English learners similar and different?
- What does it mean to "know" a language?
- How long does it take for a second language to fully develop?
- What types of instruction are effective for English learners?
- Can students learn content and language simultaneously?
- In what ways can an instructional program for English learners be structured?

Differences Among English Learners

The following factors distinguish English learners from one another (Fisher, Frey, & Rothenberg, 2008):

- **Linguistic differences**—These influence how educators can draw on their students' prior knowledge. In a community where all the English learners speak Spanish, the dominant non-English language in the United States, teachers can rely on Latin and Greek roots, which are similar in Spanish and English, for teaching new vocabulary. But cognates are far rarer between Asian languages and English. In most schools, there are numerous languages spoken, making the usefulness of cognates variable depending on the student.

- **Proficiency in the home language**—Prior education and life experiences influence acquisition of a second language, with children who possess a strong foundation in their first being better able to learn English.

- **Number of languages spoken**—Some students communicate in more than one language at home, depending on the family's traditions. English learners may be acquiring a third language, not a second.

- **Generation**—Some English learners are born in North America but have been exposed to varying degrees of their home language and English, and others may have arrived early in their lives. Older elementary students may be the most proficient English speakers at home and serve as translators for their parents. These children are sometimes described as generation 1.5 learners because of their unique language experiences as native-born children of immigrant families.

- **Poverty**—Food insecurity, housing concerns, and lack of preventive health care can negatively impact physical, psychological, and social development, making children less ready to learn a new language.

- **Motivation**—Individual differences in motivation result in differing levels of inclination to learn a new language. Make no mistake—learning a new language is hard work. A child who expects to return soon to his or her homeland may be less motivated to communicate in English.

- **Personality**—Children who are shy may be reluctant to speak and write in a language in which they feel hesitant. Students who lack confidence or who hold themselves to a high personal standard may not want to use English.

These factors combine in unique ways to form learners who display a fascinating range of behaviors and dispositions. In this chapter, we will provide an overview of the way language develops, discuss the importance of talk and academic language, and examine the curricular and instructional features of quality programs for English learners.

How a Second Language Develops

Language acquisition, even that of a first language, is complex and not fully understood. While several theoretical perspectives exist regarding initial language growth, all agree that developmental, social, and physiological elements play important roles. However, with second language acquisition, the picture is even more clouded. Most students will achieve expected milestones in their first language (L_1), but these may be somewhat delayed in their second language (L_2) due to cognitive load. Adding to this load is the content demand, since—to reiterate what Susana Dutro and Carrol Moran (2003) have said—these students are simultaneously learning English while learning *in* English.

It is apparent that the social exchanges of language precede the academic ones. The conversational fluency of the playground and the lunchroom is called *basic interpersonal communication skills* (BICS). This is the discourse of everyday social interaction between and among children and adults. Teachers tell children, "Put on your coats, and line up by the door." Children ask, "May I go to the bathroom?" The teacher observes them conversing with one another, asking questions, debating, and telling jokes. We can be easily lured into thinking that conversational fluency equates to academic language proficiency. But while BICS emerges more rapidly, academic discourse takes longer. Known as *cognitive academic language proficiency* (CALP), the verbal and written performance in L_2 takes far longer to develop.

Jim Cummins (1982) compared BICS and CALP using the metaphor of an iceberg, with BICS rising above the surface and CALP, larger but unseen, representing the vast amount of language required for true proficiency. He further described the development of these two aspects of language along a continuum of context and cognitive demand. Language that is relatively undemanding and context-embedded would include the teacher standing by the door and using beckoning gestures to instruct the students to line up. On the other hand, a discussion of a passage in a social studies textbook about the Pilgrims' desire for religious freedom is more cognitively demanding and has a reduced context, because "religious freedom" is an abstract construction. Figure 2.1 illustrates the influence of context and cognitive demand for language learners.

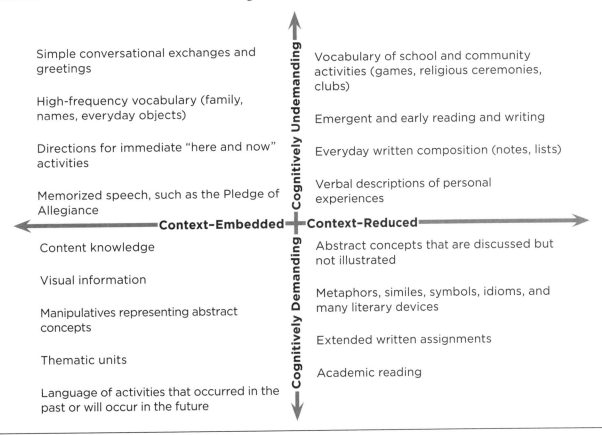

Figure 2.1: A continuum of language demands.

The key question, of course, is the length of time needed for second-language acquisition. The answer is, "It depends." The factors mentioned earlier have a strong influence on the number of years it can take to fully develop true language proficiency, including CALP. Wayne Thomas and Virginia Collier's (1997) longitudinal analysis of more than seven hundred thousand English learners found that it ranged from five to ten years, with the amount of formal education in the first language being the strongest variable. While these findings are not without their critics, most educators understand that second language development takes years. Importantly, the number of years required to develop academic language proficiency varies based on the type of instruction the student receives. Although there are a number of different program models that differ in terms of primary and secondary language instruction, those that are effective ensure that special attention is paid to oral language experiences.

The Importance of Talk

Learning occurs through language; our ability to speak makes us human. While organisms can communicate, only humans can put ideas into spoken words. Many (although not all) spoken languages have a written form as well. Written language allows us the further advantage of storing information outside of our own bodies. We don't have to memorize our history—we can write it in a book or put it on the Internet. But written forms of language begin with spoken forms, and children learning a second language need lots of opportunities to use spoken language.

How often have you gained insight into your own thinking while in the act of talking to someone else? You realize, "Yes, that's exactly what I think" as you are making a point in conversation. Although younger learners don't possess the same level of metacognitive awareness as adults, a similar process takes place in them. When students talk with one another, they clarify their own thinking even as they explain an idea to someone else.

While talk is foundational for L_2 learning, it is important to note that second language learners may be reticent about participating in whole-class discussions. In fact, when students are first introduced to a new language, they are likely to resist talking at all. This is the silent phase we referred to earlier (page 7), when the learner is attending to the sounds of the language and is not yet ready to attempt to produce the language. This silent phase does not have to last long, especially when students are provided with a safe way to practice. When we address the affective filter (Krashen, 1982) and ensure that students are not experiencing stress or anxiety about language learning, they move quickly from the silent phase to beginning language learning. Small-group and partner discussions should come before large-group discussions so that students can practice producing and listening to English in a low-risk environment.

Perhaps the most powerful message a principal can communicate to one's staff is that talk matters. We often hear from teachers that they are reluctant to have their students engage in much talk, because they believe their administrators expect the classroom to be quiet. Simply put, a quiet classroom is not necessarily a good classroom. When English learners are present, a quiet classroom is a dangerously inadequate one. Of course, the talk that students engage in should be mostly academic in nature, and teachers can structure their classrooms to ensure that students practice this type of talk.

One type of practice in academic language is the use of sentence frames. Sentence frames allow students to apprentice into language, adding their own information to forms that are consistent with the targeted language. For example, during her fourth-grade social studies lesson, Ms. Armenta provided her students with the following language frame as part of the small-group work they were doing:

This event in history reminds me of _____, because _____.

This frame encourages students to make historical and personal connections and to practice academic English. In terms of responses, students used the frame to discuss their understanding of the California Gold Rush. Some examples heard during student-to-student discussions included:

- Marcos: "This event in history reminds me of going to the casino, because people wanna get rich fast."

- Alexis: "This event in history reminds me of the Donner Party, because they moved to get a better life."

- Uriel: "This event in history reminds me of wagons, because they have those."

Figure 2.2 (page 20) shows a number of sample frames used in social studies.

Developing Academic Language and Vocabulary

The language of children broadens as they become aware of the various functions language can serve. Toddlers first learn that they can use spoken language to manage their wants and needs, and over the next few years they learn how to express emotions and ideas. Linguist M. A. K. Halliday (1975) described these language functions across seven dimensions:

1. **Instrumental**—to express needs ("Want cookie" or "I would like to call grandma.")

2. **Regulatory**—to tell others what to do ("Gimmee!" or "You can play with me.")

3. **Interactional**—to foster relationships with others ("I love you, Mama.")

4. **Personal**—to express an opinion or feeling ("I like ice cream" or "I am sad.")

5. **Imaginative**—to tell stories and jokes ("Once upon on a time . . .")

6. **Heuristic**—to solve problems ("How do you do that?")

7. **Representative**—to discuss facts and ideas ("The gold rush began in California in 1849.")

I think _____ is important, because _____.

I agree/disagree with _____, because _____.

They say _____ and/but I say _____ because _____.

Both _____,and _____ are alike/different, because _____.

According to _____, ...

After listening to _____, I found that _____.

A _____ is a symbol of _____.

_____ is famous for _____.

This event in history reminds me of _____, because _____.

This event happened because _____.

From the point of view of _____.

Due to the fact that _____ (cause), _____ (effect) happened.

_____(event) occurred before _____. (previous event)

If _____ didn't _____, then _____.

I think _____ is important, because _____ and _____.

By looking at the photograph of _____, I can predict _____ happened.

The effect of _____ was caused by _____.

Long ago they used _____, and now we use _____.

I believe _____, because _____.

Most people believe _____, but in actuality _____.

From the perspective of _____, I think/understand _____.

The cause of _____ is/are/was _____.

_____ is important to our history, because _____.

I think the point of view of the writer was _____, because _____.

If I lived in the year _____ in _____, I could _____.

Figure 2.2: Sample language frames.

An important theory in second language development, especially for beginners, is *total physical response* (TPR) (Asher, 1969). The TPR approach attempts to duplicate initial first language learning through the use of gestures, movements, and facial expressions. TPR is especially effective for relating the meaning of verbs and nouns, as well as for demonstrating familiar processes. Movements and gestures are paired with words, and students are encouraged to duplicate the movements. The first three functions of language—instrumental, regulatory, and interactional— are well suited to TPR and for this reason are commonly used with newcomers.

The last four language functions—personal, imaginative, heuristic, and representative—are especially important in the classroom. Table 2.1 contains examples of each of these functions for primary and upper grade students. Taken together, they form the basis for academic language, or what we like to call "the language of the lesson." As Cummins (1982) describes, academic language takes far longer to emerge than the language type needed for social interactions. A major challenge is that the events discussed are more abstract and exist primarily outside of the classroom. When we speak about volcanoes, we rely on supportive techniques that bring these concepts to life. It's hard to imagine teaching about lava flow without including photographs and film clips. Events of the past, like the Revolutionary War, are illustrated with reproductions from the time and are often explained using graphic organizers and other note-taking devices.

Table 2.1: Language Functions in the Elementary Classroom

Function	Primary Grades	Intermediate Grades
Personal	"I like this book, because it's about a girl like me."	"I agree with Sarai that the best thing to do now is to finish the section on volcanoes, then we can read the part about earthquakes."
Imaginative	"Once there was a talking dog, but only the boy could hear him."	"The story I am writing is about an astronaut who meets an alien when he lands on the planet Jupiter."
Heuristic	"Where's the puzzle piece that fits here?"	"I added these two fractions, but I came up with the wrong answer. What did I do wrong?"
Representational	"Firefighters protect the neighborhood."	"The colonists disguised themselves as Native Americans and threw the tea into the Boston Harbor."

Photographs, film, graphic organizers, and note-taking tools are examples of instructional methods called *specially designed academic instruction in English* (SDAIE) used to support language learners. The use of these routines is a hallmark of *sheltered English*, an older term describing content instruction for English learners. Many instructional routines are SDAIE, and these are effective for all students. However, it is useful to look at the qualities of SDAIE instruction, rather than specific activities used in the classroom. Instruction in L_2 is scaffolded with:

- **Verbal supports**—These include attention to speaking slowly and clearly, restating and rephrasing key points, and providing longer wait time for student responses to questions.

- **Visual supports**—New or unfamiliar vocabulary is featured in written as well as verbal form, images are frequently used, and real objects are furnished when appropriate. Manipulatives such as counting cubes and magnetic letters further illustrate abstract concepts.

- **Cognitive supports**—These utilize graphic organizers, thematic curriculum, teacher modeling and demonstration, and teacher think-alouds. In addition, it is clearly established at the beginning that the purpose is to alert students to the content, language, and social objectives of the lesson.

- **Background knowledge**—Oral composition precedes written composition, prior knowledge is activated, and background knowledge gaps are filled before introducing new material.

- **Interaction**—Students work frequently with partners or in small heterogeneous groups to allow students to scaffold meaning for and with one another.

- **Attention to L$_1$**—The teacher makes connections to cognates (words with a common derivation), and organizes content and instruction to reflect student experiences, cultures, and heritage.

- **Formative assessment**—The teacher checks for understanding throughout the lesson, and students are given opportunities to gauge their own learning and progress toward goals.

You can see the influence of TPR in the SDAIE approach, especially in its attention to realia (real objects), gestures, expressions, and movement. In addition, the SDAIE approach also highlights the following behaviors and practices to avoid:

- Using idioms that unnecessarily complicate the language

- Using multiple meaning words without clarifying the intended purpose

- Restricting student thinking by ruling out ideas influenced by their own cultural experiences

Schools with English learners benefit from having expert teachers who understand SDAIE methods. Some states, such as California, Texas, New York, and Florida, tie teacher licensure to formal SDAIE coursework. Many others reference English learners in their credentialing system. However, fifteen states still do not require any specialized training or preparation to teach these students (Ballantyne, Sanderman, & Levy, 2008). Of course, English learners reside in all U.S. states and territories. Even among those teachers with high levels of preparation, coaching and professional development are necessary to validate and extend their ability to provide quality instruction for English learners. This often occurs in professional learning communities (DuFour, DuFour, & Eaker, 2008) in which groups of teachers meet to analyze student work and plan quality instruction.

A widely used organizational framework for teacher support for SDAIE is the *sheltered instruction observation protocol*, more frequently called SIOP (Echevarria et al., 2010). SIOP emphasizes ongoing professional development through the use of an observation protocol to document the use of supplementary materials, enhanced instruction, and purposeful lesson delivery. These observation protocols serve as the basis for coaching conversations between teacher and mentor.

SIOP organizes quality instruction into eight areas of concentration. Each is necessary for English learners to experience success in school.

1. **Preparation:** Preparation includes identifying the content and language objectives to be shared with students, the materials to be used, and the ways in which content will be differentiated. It also includes plans for meaningful activities that allow students to practice language.

2. **Building background:** Teachers build background by establishing connections to previously taught concepts and students' experiences. In addition, they emphasize key vocabulary, so that students have multiple opportunities to use and learn the words.

3. **Comprehensible input:** Teachers create comprehensible input by using language appropriate for students' proficiency levels.

4. **Strategies:** Teachers use instructional routines strategically to scaffold students' learning, including modeling, guiding, and questioning.

5. **Interaction:** Teachers provide students, as part of their learning environment, with multiple opportunities to interact with each other and their teacher. These interactions occur in whole-class, small-group, and individual arrangements. As we have noted, ensuring that students talk every day in school, using increasingly sophisticated academic language, is the hallmark of effective practice for English learners.

6. **Practice and application:** Students are provided with hands-on materials and manipulatives so they can practice the new content knowledge as concretely as possible. These practice activities allow students to learn content while using a number of different language components, including reading, writing, speaking, listening, and viewing.

7. **Lesson delivery:** The entire lesson, including the meaningful tasks that students complete and the supplemental instruction they are provided, supports the planned content and language objectives, the pace of the lesson is appropriate for students' proficiency, and the vast majority of the students participate.

8. **Review and assessment:** As part of the lesson, the teacher reviews key vocabulary and key concepts. In addition, the teacher provides students with feedback and plans future instruction based on student performance. This feed-forward component allows teachers to be responsive to the needs of students and to plan lessons that close the gaps identified in student learning.

These eight components are critical to the success of English learners and should be used to design instruction. Our experiences suggest that having a framework in which SDAIE can be integrated, rather than planning lessons and developing separate accommodations or alternatives for English learners, helps teachers plan lessons that address all students' needs.

A Framework for Instructional Design

Effective instruction for English learners needs to be more than a hodge-podge of activities and assignments. A scripted program that doesn't take into account the many variables that make students individuals is equally damaging. Effective instruction requires a systematic approach to learning that nevertheless allows for the kind of scaffolding, individual support, differentiated instruction, and mastery learning required by all language learners.

For more than a decade, we have researched a structured approach to teaching called a *gradual release of responsibility instructional framework* (Fisher & Frey, 2007b, 2008). This approach is predicated on the work of Pearson and Gallagher (1983), who pioneered a sequence of reading instructions that includes shared, guided, and independent reading. Like its model, this instructional framework reflects a shift in cognitive responsibility from teacher to student. A major addition, and one especially important for English learners, is the collaborative learning that comes from peers. The components include:

- A *focus lesson* that is brief (five to fifteen minutes), during which time the teacher (1) establishes purpose by stating the content, language, and social objectives; (2) models or demonstrates; and (3) thinks aloud to make his or her expert thinking apparent to students

- *Guided instruction* that further scaffolds learning through the use of (1) robust questions to check for understanding (2), cognitive and metacognitive prompts, (3) cues to shift attention, and (4) direct explanation as needed when the learner isn't yet able to take on the skill or concept (Fisher & Frey, 2010a)

- *Collaborative learning* with peer partners and small groups to clarify and refine their collective understanding; this productive group work features both group and individual accountability (Frey, Fisher, & Everlove, 2009)

- *Independent learning* in and out of the classroom, which occurs only after guided and collaborative learning has taken place

Figure 2.3 illustrates this model.

We have encountered a misconception that is worth mentioning here, especially because it has implications for the principal. The misconception is that these phases of instruction must be in a prescribed order—that is, you must always begin with a focus lesson, followed immediately by guided instruction, then collaborative learning, ending with independent learning. While this is an advisable structure for building skills and conceptual knowledge, in practice it's a rare lesson that focuses on only one phase. It is far more common to have a number of skills and concepts being introduced in a staggered manner within a single lesson, with the students at varying stages of mastery.

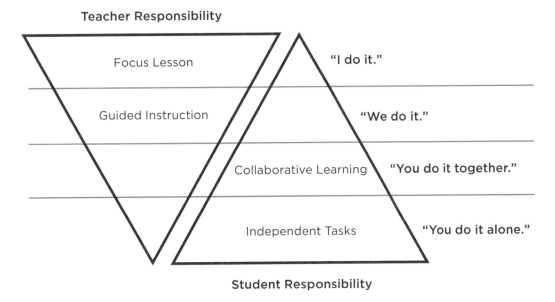

Teacher Responsibility

Focus Lesson   "I do it."

Guided Instruction   "We do it."

Collaborative Learning   "You do it together."

Independent Tasks   "You do it alone."

Student Responsibility

Source: Better Learning Through Structured Teaching: A Framework for the Gradual Release of Responsibility *(p 4), by Douglas Fisher and Nancy Frey. Alexandria, VA: ASCD. © 2008 by ASCD. Reprinted with permission. Learn more about ASCD at www.ascd.org.*

Figure 2.3: Gradual release of responsibility instructional framework.

Let's look more closely at a third-grade social studies lesson. Suppose the students are being introduced to Native American tribes that live in the region and have spent two previous lessons examining factors that contributed to and detracted from people's lives there. The students already possess knowledge of the geographic features of the region and have even deeper knowledge of the climate of the area. Thus, a lesson might begin with a brief partner discussion on the unique features of the desert geography and climate (*collaborative learning*), followed by a short writing-to-learn activity about what it would be like to live in the desert (*independent learning*). Next, the teacher establishes the purpose ("You're going to learn about the Native Americans who lived in the desert nearby") and provides direct explanation, then models and thinks aloud with a short piece of text (*focus lesson*). As students work in small groups using a simple map of the region (*collaborative learning*), the teacher moves in and out of groups, checking for understanding about the new information (*guided instruction*). The lesson ends with students adding information to a graphic organizer (*independent learning*). Importantly, the evening's homework is not about Native American tribes, because that information is too new. Instead, students are assigned the task of talking with a family member about whether he or she has visited or lived in a desert somewhere in the world (*out-of-school independent learning.*) The teacher will use this information in a discussion the following day.

The usefulness of structuring teaching using a gradual release of responsibility framework is that content and language are introduced, scaffolded, clarified, and mastered in a purposeful way. This is vital for English learners, because it accounts for possible gaps in their language and content knowledge. And because English learners must do double the work (Short & Fitzsimmons, 2007), it is also vital that content and literacy knowledge be elegantly intertwined to streamline their learning.

Content and Literacy Learning

It is not uncommon for literacy to be viewed as a subject for the reading and language arts block, with less attention paid to it during math, social studies, science, and the arts. But literacy learning—the ability to speak and listen, read, write, and view—is essential to content learning, too. Content and literacy learning go hand in hand, and neglecting one jeopardizes the other.

The adoption of the Common Core State Standards has drawn further attention to this relationship. With its emphasis on informational texts (a fifty-fifty split by fourth grade between narrative and expository), all students will be further challenged to discuss, read, and write about topics appropriate for their grade level. Ms. Wentworth's third-grade students exemplify the reciprocal nature of content and literacy in their science classroom. For weeks, this Massachusetts class of English learners had been closely reading *A Drop of Water* (Wick, 1997) and had conducted related science experiments on water's varying states, including condensation on the classroom windows and steam rising from their teacher's mug of tea. One snowy morning, Ms. Wentworth's students bundled up, and she took them outside to examine snowflakes. Partners caught snowflakes as they fell, using a toothpick to transfer them to a mirror. "Look through the magnifying glass to examine your snowflake," Ms. Wentworth reminded the class, "then describe it to your partner. Be sure to talk like scientists." The children had learned the vocabulary of snowflakes, especially terms such as *angle* and *branches* to refer to snowflake structures, as well as descriptive terms like *crystal clear* and *lacy*. As the teacher listened in, Roel told Tino, "There are six branches, and it's mostly white. The edges on this one are broke . . ."

"Say *broken*," Tino told him.

"Yeah, the edges is . . . are broken," Roel continued.

After the students returned to the classroom, Ms. Wentworth opened *A Drop of Water* and turned to the pages on snowflakes. She displayed it on the document camera so all the children could see the text and photographs.

"I heard several of you using scientific terms like *ice crystal* and *water molecule* when you talked to your partners," she said. "Let's look again at one of the books we've been reading so we can compare that information to what we just saw outside. We've read this before."

After the students looked at their books, Ms. Wentworth continued, "Now let's look again for how the author uses words to help us understand snowflakes. Then we'll write our findings using our scientific language and the information the author gave us." She read: "The angles between the six branches are repeated over and over again in many of the smaller details of this amazing structure. How can such an intricate object form in the sky?" (p. 28), and then, a few sentences later, "Sometimes snow mixes with pellets of sleet, which are frozen raindrops like the ones shown below." Ms. Wentworth then gestured to the photograph on the screen. "By contrast, snowflakes are ice crystals that form when water vapor changes directly from a gas to a solid" (p. 28).

The teacher then spoke about her own comprehension. "When the author said 'by contrast,' it really helped me remember that he was comparing snowflakes and sleet. Which did you observe outside? Talk with your partner about your observations."

Roel and Tino looked at the photographs while discussing whether theirs had been a damaged snowflake or sleet. "It had six branches, so I think it's a snowflake," said Roel.

"I do, too," said Tino, "but maybe it got hitted by something on the way down to us."

Ms. Wentworth gestured to a paper on their desks. "You've got an observation sheet in front of you," she said. "I'd like each of you to sketch what you saw, then use words to describe it. Finally, write your conclusion about whether you saw sleet or snowflakes. Make sure you write like a scientist, and use words we've been learning to explain your thinking."

In the course of a forty-minute science lesson, Ms. Wentworth incorporated many of the elements of effective literacy instruction into content learning (table 2.2). She modeled thinking aloud during text reading, especially in showing her students how text is used for consultative purposes. She designed a motivating activity to build background knowledge, pairing students to support one another's expressive language. And she frontloaded vocabulary, incorporated writing, and made sure that she stayed close to her students, so she would know what needed to be taught next. These elements of literacy instruction are purposeful in their own right, as they advance students' ability to use spoken and written language to learn content. By foregrounding the language of the lesson, students are learning to incorporate both the content knowledge as well as the means to think, talk, and write about it.

Table 2.2: Key Elements of Effective Literacy Instruction

Instructional Practice	Explanation	Focus on EL
Direct, explicit comprehension instruction	Teach the strategies and processes that proficient readers use to understand what they read.	Model, model, model! Amplify instruction rather than simplify.
Effective instructional principles embedded in content	Use content-area texts in the language arts block and teach content-area-specific reading and writing skills in content.	Use content as a vehicle to teach language. Students do not learn language in a vacuum. Incorporate language teaching throughout the day, throughout the content areas, to accelerate learning.
Motivation and self-directed learning	Build students' motivation to read and learn, and provide them with the instruction and supports needed for independent learning tasks.	Teach students to take responsibility for learning and re-engage as active, not passive, learners. Provide choice in text selection. Provide multileveled texts on a topic.
Text-based collaborative learning	Encourage students to interact with one another around a variety of texts.	Group students heterogeneously to provide language models and scaffolds for learning when students are working with one another in collaborative tasks.
Strategic tutoring	Provide students with intense individualized reading, writing, and content instruction as needed.	Group students homogeneously to address like needs and develop language proficiency when the teacher is present.

continued →

Instructional Practice	Explanation	Focus on EL
Diverse texts	Use texts at a variety of difficulty levels and on a variety of topics.	Ensure access for ELs through differentiated texts that address the same topic. Incorporate texts from a variety of cultural perspectives.
Intensive writing instruction	Connect to the kinds of writing tasks students will have to perform across the school year.	Assign tasks that require high-level critical thinking skills, and teach the language and strategies needed to analyze, synthesize, justify, persuade, and so on. Scaffold writing instruction through a gradual release of responsibility.
Technology	Use technology as a tool for and a topic of literacy instruction.	Use technology to scaffold understanding through visuals and a variety of sources.
Ongoing formative assessment	Learn how students are progressing under current instructional practices.	Assess all four domains of language—reading, writing, speaking, and listening.

Source: Adapted from Language Learners in the English Classroom, *by Douglas Fisher, Carol Rothenberg, and Nancy Frey. © 2007, National Council of Teachers of Education. Reprinted with permission.*

Instructional Programs for English Learners

A number of different instructional program models have been developed for the delivery of quality instruction for English learners. This is a politically charged, often ideological discussion about what represents the best program for English learners. Of course, there are good and bad examples of each type.

Having said that, we have organized our discussion into four program categories (table 2.3). We acknowledge that not all of the program types listed are available as an option in each school system. The reality is that schools make program model decisions based on a number of factors, including the number of students they serve, the variety of languages that teachers and students speak, state laws, and district policies. As an example, it's easier to organize a bilingual program when the school or district enrolls students who speak Spanish and English. It's harder to have a bilingual program when the students speak Hmong, Vietnamese, Arabic, Oromo, and ten other languages.

Table 2.3: Programs for English Learners

Program	Language of Instruction	Educational Objective
Dual-immersion bilingual	L_1 and L_2 use are segmented.	Develop L_1 and acquire L_2.
Transitional/early-exit bilingual	English rapidly increases in kindergarten as L_2 is faded.	L_2 becomes the language of instruction in first or second grade.
Late-exit bilingual	English increases more gradually as L_2 is faded.	L_2 becomes the language of instruction by the end of sixth grade.
English immersion	Instruction is in English only.	Acquire L_2.

Dual-Immersion Bilingual

In this model, students are taught in two languages for many years, though the percentage of each language used for instruction can change (Quintanar-Sarellana, 2004). Typically, in a dual-immersion classroom, about half the students speak one of the two languages at home and the other half speak the other language at home. For example, in Mr. Jimenez's fourth-grade class, sixteen of the students speak English at home and fifteen speak Spanish at home. He teaches science in English and social studies in Spanish, and then every three weeks reverses them. For language arts, he teaches in both Spanish and English each day, scaffolding students' understanding of the ways the two languages work. He wants his students to develop their ability to code-switch and translate their ideas between Spanish and English quickly, so he models this as part of his instruction. Knowing that his students have the background knowledge to master mathematics, he always teaches it in Spanish.

Transitional or Early-Exit Bilingual

In this model, students are supported with their primary language, but the goal is to transition them to English instruction as quickly as possible. Typically, instruction in kindergarten in a transitional program starts with 80–90 percent primary language instruction. This percentage is reduced in the first year as well as in subsequent years. Students are transitioned to English instruction early in elementary school, usually by first or second grade. Advocates of this model suggest that, although students need primary language support, the goal is English proficiency, and English has to become the language of instruction early in the learner's life. For example, during the first part of her kindergarten year, Mariana learned the names of common items in the environment in English, but was taught in Spanish. By January of that year, Mariana was being taught 50 percent in Spanish and 50 percent in English. She exited the bilingual program in second grade. Although her scores in English were depressed at that time, she did perform well in English by fourth grade. Her Spanish language proficiency was maintained by her parents and the after-school program, including a middle school class called Spanish for Spanish Speakers.

Late-Exit Bilingual

In this model, students are taught in two languages through at least elementary school. Typically, all of the students in a late-exit bilingual program speak the same heritage or home language. The goal of this program model is to develop proficiency in both languages; it is often thought of as an "additive approach." As with all bilingual models, there must be sufficient numbers of students to create a class, known as the critical mass requirement, and there must be a teacher who can teach in two languages. For example, Ms. Uribe teaches a second-grade late-exit bilingual class in which 60 percent of the instruction is in Spanish and 40 percent is in English. The students in Ms. Uribe's class all speak Spanish at home. By fifth grade, the instruction will shift to 60 percent English and 40 percent Spanish, which is consistent with the goal of developing students' proficiency in both languages.

As another example, Mr. Nguyen teaches a late-exit bilingual class in Vietnamese. He teaches students in grades 4 and 5, which were combined in order to obtain critical mass. His students learn in both languages and have the same teacher for two years. They had one teacher for kindergarten and first grade, another teacher for second and third grade, and now Mr. Nguyen. Again, the goal is to ensure biliteracy.

English Immersion

This program model has a number of different names, including structured English immersion and mainstream English cluster. In this model, students are taught in English for the vast majority of the day. (People who question the effectiveness of this program model call it *submersion* and see it as a replacement model [Ramirez & Merino, 1990]). In an immersion classroom, there may be some explanations or responses to questions in the student's home language, but instruction is provided in English. There may also be paraprofessionals who speak the languages that the students speak who can provide directions and support as needed. This is the default program for students who speak languages for which there is not a critical mass, as well as the default model for states that forbid bilingual education. In addition, it is a model chosen by some families that want their children to learn as fast as possible in English.

In any case, the immersion classroom provides students with academic language instruction in addition to the regular class instruction. This is often called *English language development* (ELD) or *English as a second language* (ESL) time, and is used to supplement the regular learning environment. In some classrooms or schools, students are regrouped for ELD/ESL at the grade level. For example, Mauricio was enrolled in an English immersion class in elementary school. His instruction was in English, mostly from monolingual English teachers. He often asked questions in Spanish and received support from his peers through language brokers in order to understand instructions. For his ELD time, he was grouped with students from other classrooms with a similar proficiency level. These ELD lessons lasted thirty minutes and focused on language acquisition. More information about ELD/ESL lessons, irrespective of where they are used, can be found in chapter 4 (page 43).

Conclusion

Creating a quality instructional program for English learners is a complex task. It requires an understanding of the differences between students as well as the ways in which language develops. It also demands that students use academic language in the classroom on a regular basis. Furthermore, it assumes that teachers understand the components of effective instruction, from planning lessons to ensuring comprehensible input for students. In teaching English learners, principals and teachers must ensure that students are provided with daily content objectives—purposes for their learning—as well as modeling, guided instruction, collaborative learning activities, and independent learning tasks. These components can be integrated into a number of different instructional programs and models, but each of them requires attention to students' learning. Part of the way that teachers pay attention to students' learning is through assessment systems, which is where we turn our attention next.

Assessing the Performance of English Learners

Issues of accountability and assessment have become part of the daily discourse of principals. In fact, you may have turned to this chapter first, because you believed it unthinkable to separate the discussion of English learner issues from the measurement of their progress. For much of the history of education in the United States, however, that was not the case. Despite the fact that the United States consists of immigrants and their descendants, English language acquisition was viewed as an imperative for the child but not necessarily for the school. However, a series of court cases and statutes have shifted the responsibility to give assessment a prominent role.

Two Court Cases and a Federal Law

It's hard to imagine that there was a time when English learners were not able to receive specialized English instruction. Yet less than forty years ago, students who did not speak English were not certain to find such services in their neighborhood public schools. A Supreme Court ruling, *Lau v. Nichols* (1974), changed that. This class-action suit, brought on behalf of a group of Chinese-speaking students in the San Francisco Unified School District, charged that nearly two-thirds of these students received no specialized instruction to develop English language skills. Even worse, access to content instruction required mastery of English! The court found in favor of the students, ruling that simply being instructed in English without necessary supports for learning did not constitute an equal education. This case

Big Idea

Assessment for English learners requires attention to the whole child. A multidimensional approach is necessary in order for a true picture to emerge. This requires balancing large-scale assessments with individualized informal ones that highlight strengths, rather than simply catalog deficits.

Questions Principals Ask

- Haven't English learners always been assessed?
- What role do screening tools, benchmark assessments, and large-scale testing play in the education of English learners?
- How are formative assessments used to improve programs?
- What are reasonable accommodations for English learners on standardized tests?

had a profound effect on the education of English learners. The program examples in the previous chapter, including English language development time in an English immersion program, are a direct outgrowth of this ruling.

A number of court cases flowed from this ruling, perhaps most significantly one by a Texas parent. Roy Castañada charged that his children were being segregated due to language and that the district failed to provide a reasonable program to educate them. An appeals court found in his favor, requiring that districts meet the following three-part test of programs (*Castañada v. Pickard*, 1981):

1. The school is pursuing a program informed by an educational theory recognized as sound by some experts in the field or, at least, deemed legitimate experimental strategy;

2. The program and practices actually used by (the) school system are reasonably calculated to implement effectively the educational theory adopted by the school;

3. The school's program succeeds, after a legitimate trial, in producing results indicating that the language barriers confronting students are actually being overcome.

This court case and the laws that flowed from it further challenged schools to not only provide a quality program for English learners and devote adequate resources to it, but also to measure its effectiveness. Importantly, a program must be discontinued if it is found to be ineffective. The *Castañada v. Pickard* ruling guides current English learner policy at the federal level.

The renewal of Elementary and Secondary Education Act (ESEA) in 2001 represented another major change in assessments for English learners. Later known as No Child Left Behind, this law mandated that all states assess students annually for English language proficiency. While some states had been doing this for many years, others had to develop such a test and have collaborated with other states to do so. The largest of these, World-Class Instructional Design and Assessment Consortium (WIDA), counts twenty-four states and the District of Columbia as members. ESEA also required all states to develop annual measurable achievement objectives to gauge the progress of English learners as a group from year to year, holding schools and districts accountable on measures of annual yearly progress.

Consider the sweep of legislation that has emerged in the last four decades. As a profession, we have come far from the days when students who spoke Chinese were denied assistance in learning a new language. *Castañada v. Pickard* (1981) drew the country's attention to the importance of both programming and its measurement, to ensure that there was a way to gauge progress. And with ESEA of 2001, English learner issues took center stage, with assessment required at the individual level and in large-scale accountability measures.

However, it's one thing to require assessment, another to do it with an acceptable level of accuracy and usefulness. As language acquisition becomes more fully understood, best practices in assessment are bound to change as well. For many schools, screening is the first assessment practice used to identify children who may profit from early intervention. While these results should be used only for preliminary identification, in some cases they carry more weight than they should.

Screening Tools

At the beginning of each school year, schools should administer screening tools to determine which students have arrived already in need of additional support and instruction. We like to think of these tools as hearing or vision screenings in that they are designed to rapidly assess large numbers of students. In most schools, a number of generic screening tools are in use. For example, it is common for schools to screen all students using such assessments such as Dynamic Indicators of Basic Early Literacy Skills (DIBELS), Developmental Reading Assessment (DRA), and the Gates-MacGinitie Reading Test (GMRT) (Beavers, 1999).

Checklists

Teams should work together to agree on which screening tools they will use. This provides teachers with an opportunity to discuss results and interventions as part of their professional learning communities and to set overall expectations for the school as part of a continuous improvement effort. Use the Essential Task List for Screening Tools (page 40 and online at **go.solution-tree.com /ELL**) as a checklist for selecting and using screening tools. We have found this generic tool very helpful in guiding discussions about appropriate screening tools for English learners.

Checklists provide teachers with a list of intended behaviors or skills against which student performance is evaluated. They are often used as quick screening tools as well. For example, most kindergarten teachers use a letter recognition checklist to determine which students know their upper and lowercase letters and which do not. This tool is helpful for screening students whose primary language does not rely on the Roman alphabet—languages such as Farsi, Russian, Vietnamese, or Chinese. It is less helpful for English learners who already use Roman letters, such as speakers of Spanish and French.

School districts also create checklists to use with English learners. For example, to screen for auditory comprehension, a district in southern California asks teachers to show students pictures and then say:

1. "Show me a truck" [three graphics of objects/nouns].

2. "Show me a hand" [three photographs of body parts].

3. "Which one is 6:30" [three clock faces]?

4. "Which one is 40 cents" [three amounts of change]?

5. "Show me running" [photographs of three activities].

6. "Show me reading" [photographs of three activities].

Oral Language Observation

Another useful screening tool focuses on students' oral language production. The tool we use most often for screening oral language development informally is the *student oral language observation matrix* (SOLOM). This tool has proven to be a useful guide for evaluating oral language proficiency as observed in a school setting (Peregoy & Boyle, 1997). It can be used to determine English acquisition phase, identify student needs, and record the progress of individuals and groups. And because it is not based on developmental milestones, it is appropriate for both the elementary and secondary levels.

The SOLOM has five scales—comprehension, fluency, vocabulary, pronunciation, and grammar—for rating key dimensions of oral language from one to five, yielding a total score that can range from five to twenty-five. A reproducible student oral language observation matrix can be found on page 41. To administer the SOLOM, students are observed in several different classroom activities in which they are interacting with the teacher or classmates, such as cooperative group tasks. On each occasion, the teacher marks rankings on the matrix according to his or her impressions of the student's use of English. Some teachers audio-record one or more of the sessions to review and confirm impressions or to examine patterns of errors or usage. The SOLOM yields ratings for four phases of English language proficiency, culminating in phase 4, full proficiency.

> **Phase 1** = 5–11
>
> **Phase 2** = 12–18
>
> **Phase 3** = 19–24
>
> **Phase 4** = 25

Commercially Available Screening Tools

There are also some newer, commercial screening tools useful with English learners. For example, the W-APT, which stands for the WIDA-ACCESS Placement Test™, is used by educators to measure the English language proficiency of students who have recently arrived in the United States. It can help determine whether or not a child is in need of English language instructional services and, if so, at what level. This tool has to be purchased from WIDA directly (www.wida.us). Here we will simply note that, while screening tools specific to the needs of EL students are difficult to find, good ones are tremendously helpful as the first step in identifying students who might need specific attention. We think of these tools as a means of putting students on our radar. Keep in mind, however, that these screening instruments are a snapshot in time and give us only a static image of who that student is.

Progress Monitoring

To extend the snapshot metaphor further, progress monitoring introduces movement to a still photograph, giving us a way of viewing the student across a period of time. The assessments used as part of progress monitoring help teachers determine if students are benefiting from classroom instruction and interventions. The reproducible Essential Task List for Progress Monitoring in Tier 1 (page 42) provides a progress-monitoring checklist. As with screening tools, there are a number of generic progress-monitoring tools available for all students.

Benchmark Assessments

More formal progress-monitoring tools given every six to ten weeks across an entire school or district are commonly called *benchmark assessments*. They provide a way for teachers and administrators to view the progress of a group of students in order to make midcourse corrections.

Benchmark assessments have been increasing in popularity. The practice of gauging progress throughout the year has a great deal of appeal, and some go so far as to say that it serves as a student motivator that can have a positive effect on achievement. While the evidence of this last claim is not clear, the fact is that, in most school districts, benchmark assessments have become routine across classrooms. For example, the Gates-MacGinitie Reading Test and Developmental Reading Assessment are often administered two or three times per year, and the results are used to make instructional decisions. In addition, information about progress monitoring is rapidly expanding. The National Center on Student Progress Monitoring, sponsored by the U.S. Office of Special Education Programs (OSEP), provides an array of free, web-based progress-monitoring resource materials at www.studentprogress.org.

The usefulness of benchmark assessments is dependent on what is done with them. Without analysis of the results, benchmarks amount to little more than an academic exercise. However when the results are used to foster conversations within and across grade levels, these assessments can be a starting point for programmatic and instructional decision making. Used well, they can play a key role in data-driven decisions.

For example, first-grade teachers at Rio Segundo Elementary School used midyear benchmark assessment data in mathematics to discuss the progress of their students. An analysis of the results showed that many of their English learners were having difficulty identifying even and odd numbers. This led to a conversation about the differences the teachers were observing between students' classroom performance, which was good, and their paper-and-pencil tasks, where they performed less well. One teacher noted that the decontextualized nature of the benchmark test was unfamiliar to all the students, but that it was especially taxing for her English learners. The teachers agreed that familiarity with the format of test items could be integrated into their classroom instruction. They decided to include written questions in their lessons so that students could become more familiar with the written forms of math vocabulary and the more formal style of questioning used. "We're not teaching to the test," said one teacher, "but we do need to be teaching them to be test-wise." Another added, "Testing is a genre, and it's important that we make sure all of our students get experience using it well to show what they know."

Formative Assessments

Although benchmark assessments serve as checkpoints throughout the year, they are not specific enough for daily teaching decisions. For that, teachers use a collection of formative assessments. These everyday methods of gathering information about student learning are the basis for informed teaching.

The practice of gauging incremental progress in learning is a hallmark of responsive teaching. This is especially important when teaching English learners, whose attentive demeanor can belie the confusion they are experiencing. These practices include (Fisher & Frey, 2007a):

- *Oral language experiences* that provide the teacher with a sense of what students know and do not know

- *Robust questions* that cause students to consider what they know and why they know it

- *Written tasks* that give students the chance to put academic vocabulary and language to more formal use

- *Projects and performances* that challenge students to apply what they have learned in creative and original ways

- *Tests* of content knowledge of the chapter or unit being studied, to gauge student mastery of the skills most recently taught

Of course, it is almost impossible to determine whether any of these are being used for the purpose of formative assessment. That requires conversation with the teacher. When observing a classroom, look for the opportunities for formative assessment, and ask the teacher whether the information is being collected and for what purpose. A simple question—"How will you know when they have learned what you are teaching?"—can get the discussion going. This can be of particular value to novice teachers who may not yet be skilled at capitalizing on the abundance of assessment information around them.

Consensus Scoring

Consensus scoring is most frequently used to examine student responses to writing prompts. The third-grade team at Abraham Lincoln Elementary meets quarterly for this purpose. After administering a timed-writing prompt the previous week asking students to describe a place where they feel happy, each teacher brought copies of three samples (with names removed) for the team to read and discuss. After scoring the number of words, number of sentences, and average sentence length, the team discussed holistic qualities such as voice, clarity, and organization of ideas. The result of this meeting provided the teachers with a sense of how the grade's writing had developed since the last consensus scoring meeting, as well as what elements would need further emphasis.

Common Assessments

Like consensus scoring, common assessments are increasingly used with grade levels to tune instructional practice. They are useful for such testing formats as multiple-choice and short-answer items. Also like consensus-scoring instruments, they are developed collaboratively by the teachers using them and are administered at an agreed point in time. After grading the assessment, teachers meet to look for patterns among incorrect items. Fifth-grade teachers at Fairfield Elementary have incorporated this practice in their grade-level meetings. After each science and social studies chapter or unit test, they run the statistics for each response. A question asking students whether a heavier object would fall faster than a lighter object drew an incorrect response rate of 71 percent, despite a lab experience designed to prove the contrary. The teachers agreed that this concept was simply too important to leave behind and designed another lesson to address this misconception directly, rather than leave it for the students to deduce.

Consensus scoring and common assessments change the unit of analysis from a single classroom to grade level. Teachers have precious little time to discuss their practices in any detail, and these approaches can shine a spotlight on the collective wisdom of the group. Analysis of student work and response patterns can give teachers the springboard for collaboration.

Large-Scale Assessments

In addition to the benchmarks and formative assessments teachers use to ensure that English learners continue to make progress, districts and states require that all students participate in large-scale assessments for accountability. As part of standards-based reform efforts, including federal laws such as the No Child Left Behind Act (2008), students learning English must participate in state accountability assessments, and schools are held accountable for their achievement. Since schools are being judged on the progress of all students, when English learners become a significant subpopulation and fail to achieve the expected results, the school as a whole can be judged as failing to make progress.

The accountability tests used in most states require a sophisticated understanding of language. Even instructions like "simplify the expression" can be ambiguous. As a result, "ELLs are under-assessed in the sense that much of what they know and much of what they [are able to] do is not captured in current assessment methods" (La Celle-Peterson & Rivera, 1994, p. 69). Simply said, a student may know the content but not yet have the language necessary to understand the question or the range of choices. This is borne out in research evidence, summarized by David Francis, Mabel Rivera, Nonie Lesaux, Michael Kieffer, & Hector Rivera (2006, p. 13):

> When faced with a large-scale test in English, an ELL must direct more cognitive resources to processing the language of the test compared to a student who is fully proficient in English. Therefore, the ELL will have fewer resources available to attend to the content being tested.

Unfortunately, principals cannot simply declare that English learners can use accommodations, unless they are sanctioned by the district or state.

We have found that it is helpful for teachers to provide students with intentional instruction focused on the common terms used on these types of assessments. Following are the meanings of some of these more common terms (Frey & Fisher, 2007):

- **Analyze**—Break the subject into parts and discuss each part.

- **Approximate**, **estimate**—Make a reasonable guess using the information that has been given.

- **Characterize**, **identify**, **explain**, **describe**—Name the characteristics that make something special, and make sure you provide a lot of details and evidence.

- **Choose the best answer**—Select the answer that is the most correct, even though it might not be totally right.

- **Chronological order**—Put events in the sequence in which they happened.

- **Comment**—Give your opinion, and support it with facts or evidence.

- **Compare**—Tell how two or more things are similar.

- **Contrast**—Tell how two or more things are different.

- **Discuss**—Tell all you can about the topic in the time you have.

- **Evaluate**—Give evidence for each side of an issue, draw conclusions from the evidence, and make a judgment about the topic.

- **Examine**—Look carefully at similar answers, as one will be a better choice.

- **Fill in the blank; complete the sentence**—If a list of possible answers is given, use the best word from the list. If not, use a word you know that best fits the meaning of the sentence.

- **Interpret**—Explain the meaning using your ideas and evidence.

- **Justify**—Provide evidence to support your answer.

- **Name, list, mention**—Give the information provided, but be brief.

- **Put in your own words**—Rewrite the complicated language in everyday language.

- **Rank**—List the information in some special order, like importance, value, or time.

- **Skim**—Glance through the passage quickly, looking for answers to specific questions.

- **State**—Give a short, simple answer. No discussion is necessary.

- **Summarize**—Briefly restate the information, and be sure to include the main points. Leave out the small details. Your answer should be shorter than the original.

- **Trace**—Give the major points in chronological order.

When English learners know these terms, they'll have a chance on the large-scale assessment. Of course, understanding the instructions is just the first part of students' success in large-scale assessments. They also have to have been taught the content in ways that ensure lasting understanding. As we discussed in chapter 2 (page 15), this requires that the instruction be comprehensible and that responsibility be released to students. It also requires significant scaffolding. But even with that level of instructional support, another issue facing English learners on large-scale assessments is fatigue. Working in a foreign language for long, uninterrupted periods of time is exhausting. When students get tired, they give up. To address this issue, students need to build their stamina. This can occur through some simple classrooms routines, such as independent reading.

If students cannot read in English for twenty to thirty minutes at a time, they will have virtually no chance of reading the comprehension passages commonly found on accountability tests. Daily independent reading builds not only content knowledge but also stamina.

In addition, English learners must be taught to take short breaks during long testing situations. They can put their heads down for a few minutes, then get back to work. If students do not know that they can do this, then they are likely to work until they are at a point of no return. In the schools where we work, we practice these short, self-initiated breaks so students know that they can use them on test days.

Finally, some supports and accommodations available during tests may ensure that English learners participate. The term *accommodation*, in fact, encompasses alterations to standard test administration procedures, including, but not limited to, how the assessment is presented to the student, how the student is allowed to respond, any equipment or materials to be used, the extent of time allowed to complete the test, and changes to the environment in which the student takes the test (Rivera, Collum, Willner, & Sia, 2006). Although this is an ever-changing area, with modifications to laws and regulations coming fast and furious, English learners have thus far been permitted very few accommodations or modifications when they participate in large-scale assessments. Again, each state, and each large-scale assessment, has guidelines for the use of accommodations for English learners. As leaders, it's our responsibility to advocate for those accommodations and to ensure that students receive those they are entitled to.

Conclusion

The laws regarding English learner education have influenced state and federal policies, and while the details may vary, the overall trend is that the progress of students should be monitored closely. Importantly, when progress is found to be inadequate, the program should be revised. Progress monitoring occurs across several dimensions, such as large-scale tests and benchmark assessments that measure groups. In addition, classroom teachers can use formative assessment practices to check for an individual student's understanding. Consensus scoring and common assessments bridge these two worlds by coupling progress among groups with next steps in instructional planning.

Essential Task List for Screening Tools

In the second column, write the name of the individual or the names of the team members who will assume responsibility for the task identified in the first column. In the third column, write the deadline for, or status of, the task.

Task	Responsible Individual(s)	Status
Review your screening instrument's items to be certain that content is aligned with the curriculum for each grade level.		
Once a tool has been selected, determine and secure the resources required to implement it.		
Determine initial professional development needs and continuing professional development support.		
Administer the screening measure three times a year (for example, early fall, midterm, and late spring).		
Create a database that aligns with the screening instrument to hold student information and scores.		
Organize the screening results (graphs and tables, for example) to provide profiles and comparisons of all students.		
Monitor results at the classroom level, and make decisions about when teachers or instructional programs require more scrutiny and support.		
Add screening results to a database so that students' performance can be monitored over time.		
Specify written steps to follow when further scrutiny is needed for students judged to be at risk.		

Source: Responsiveness to Intervention (RTI): How to Do It, by Evelyn Johnson, Daryl F. Mellard, Doug Fuchs, and Melinda A. McKnight. © 2006, National Research Center on Learning Disabilities. Used with permission.

Student Oral Language Observation Matrix

Based on your observation, mark with an "X" in each category the trait that best describes the English learner's abilities.

Traits	1	2	3	4	5
Comprehension	Cannot understand even simple conversation	Has difficulty with what is said; comprehends only social conversation spoken slowly with frequent repetitions	Understands most of what is said at slower-than-normal speed with repetitions	Understands nearly everything at normal speed, although occasional repetition may be necessary	Understands everyday conversation and normal classroom discussions without difficulty
Fluency	Speaks in such a halting and fragmentary way as to make conversation virtually impossible	Usually hesitates; often forced into silence by language limitations	Frequently interrupts speech in everyday conversation and classroom discussion to search for the correct manner of expression	Generally speaks fluently in everyday conversation and classroom discussion with occasional lapses to search for the correct manner of expression	Speaks fluently and effortlessly in everyday conversation and classroom discussions, approximating a native speaker
Vocabulary	Has vocabulary limitations so extreme as to make conversation virtually impossible	Misuses words and has very limited vocabulary, making comprehension quite difficult	Frequently uses wrong words and has inadequate vocabulary, making conversation somewhat limited	Occasionally uses inappropriate terms or must rephrase ideas because of lexical inadequacies	Uses vocabulary and idioms like a native speaker
Pronunciation	Has pronunciation problems so severe as to make speech virtually unintelligible	Cannot be understood because of pronunciation problems and must frequently repeat	Has pronunciation problems that require listener concentration and occasionally lead to misunderstanding	Is always intelligible, though speaks with an accent and occasionally uses inappropriate intonation patterns	Pronounces and intones words like a native speaker
Grammar	Makes errors in grammar and word order so severe as to make speech virtually unintelligible	Makes grammar and word order errors that make comprehension difficult; must often rephrase or restrict self to basic patterns	Makes frequent errors of grammar and word order that occasionally obscure meaning	Occasionally makes grammatical or word-order errors that do not obscure meaning	Grammatical usage and word order approximate that of a native speaker

Essential Task List for Progress Monitoring in Tier 1

In the second column, write the name of the individual or the names of the team members who will assume responsibility for the task in the first column. In the third column, write the deadline for or status of the task.

Task	Responsible Individual(s)	Timeline/Status
Within the relevant content area, review the progress-monitoring measure or tool selected for Tier 1 to determine whether content is aligned with your curriculum.		
Once a tool has been selected, determine and secure the resources required to implement it (for example, computers, folders or copies, testing areas).		
Determine initial professional development needs and continuing professional development support.		
Implement a system of data collection and progress monitoring that includes determining both level and growth rate.		
Administer the progress-monitoring measure frequently enough to assess a learner's responsiveness. At Tier 1, screening is three times a year, with routine monitoring weekly or twice weekly.		
Monitor results at the individual student level and make decisions about reasonable cut scores to determine movement to Tier 2 and beyond.		
Monitor results at the classroom level and make decisions about when teachers or instructional programs require more scrutiny and support.		

Source: Responsiveness to Intervention (RTI): How to Do It, *by Evelyn Johnson, Daryl F. Mellard, Doug Fuchs, and Melinda A. McKnight. © 2006, National Research Center on Learning Disabilities. Used with permission.*

Intervening for English Learner Performance

The debate about the effects of accountability systems has produced one wide area of agreement—it has drawn overdue attention to the progress of students with learning and language differences. The shorthand of accountability-speak is that these groups comprise "significant subgroups"—that is, students whose socioeconomic, ethnic, language, and disability differences warrant our attention. However, any principal knows that the broad categories of significant subgroups can obscure the uniqueness of their members.

The truth of this is perhaps no more apparent than with English learners. As discussed in chapter 1, each student learning another language brings a singular mix of experiences in and out of school. A young child's exposure to his or her first language, previous school experiences, cultural traditions, and age of introduction to English all have a profound effect on that child's progress in English. For this reason, progress must be considered in relation to that of a child's true peers.

Big Idea

Response to instruction and intervention (RTI[2]) with English learners is complex because of the many factors that influence second language development. English learners deserve supplemental and intensive interventions, especially when their performance pales in compares with that of true peers, not just chronological ones.

Questions Principals Ask

- What are true peers?
- What is RTI[2]?
- What elements are necessary in quality core instruction?
- Is English language development (ELD) the same as Tier 2?
- What does intensive intervention at Tier 3 look like?
- Does my district have a problem with disproportionality in special education?

Who Are a Student's True Peers?

There was a time in the United States when those who did not know English were segregated and marginalized in our schooling system. In fact, decades before the landmark *Brown v. Board of Education* ruling by the 1954 Supreme Court brought an end to the shameful practice of racial segregation, families of Mexican descent won the first desegregation case in the country. What became known as the Lemon Grove Incident of 1930 took place in a farming community outside of San Diego, California, when the local school board attempted to send Spanish-speaking children to a separate school that was literally on the other side of the railroad tracks. On the first day of school, the principal stood at the schoolhouse door and refused admittance to any child of Mexican descent, directing them instead to an old building. The parents refused to send their children to *la caballeriza* (the stable) and filed a lawsuit against the school board. The parents won the case, and in March of 1931, their children were readmitted to Lemon Grove Grammar School (Alvarez, 1986).

We tell this story as a reminder of how bewildering such policies seem when viewed over the distance of time. It is hard to imagine an elementary principal barring the schoolhouse door. It's even more painful to think that there was a time when exclusion was the rule of the day. And yet more subtle practices of exclusion continue to linger. It is not uncommon to find some who think that assimilation is the only goal for educating English learners. We have personally witnessed otherwise responsible teachers admonishing students for speaking in their home language, even in private conversation. And perhaps most bewildering of all, we have seen professionals list all of the factors that make an English learner unique but then compare them only to monolingual peers and find them deficient.

The National Center for Culturally Responsive Educational Systems (NCCREST) defines *true peers* as those with "similar language proficiencies, culture, and experiential backgrounds" (Brown & Doolittle, 2008, p. 6). Determining who the true peers are requires a nuanced look at the progress of students at your school. While state and federal achievement reports classify English learners as a monolithic group and compare their growth against a standard, these numbers do little more than alert educators and communities to a problem. At the school level, the progress of individual students must be further examined in the context of the local cohort of true peers. Brown and Doolittle (2008) go on to advise that "if several 'true peers' are struggling, this is an indication that the instruction is less than optimal for that group of students" (p. 6).

When groups of true peers fail to make progress, it is a clarion call letting us know that, however well intended, the current curricular and instructional program is not effective in its present state. This can be a difficult and sensitive topic for caring educators, as the level of effort and commitment to student learning can be high even when achievement is not. Having said that, it is equally important to look beyond national norms when gauging student progress. It is unlikely that a second-grade English learner at the early intermediate phase of language development is going to have the same achievement profile as the native English-speaking classmate sitting next to her. The norms established to measure fluency, for instance, are not able to account for the language development differences between the two girls. A second analysis of the student's progress compared to linguistically similar students is warranted. If her progress is still found wanting, increased intervention is indicated.

In this chapter, we will discuss topics related to instruction and intervention for English learners. We will begin with response to instruction and intervention (RTI²), with discussion about the curricular and personnel elements involved at each tier. We describe variables that can be manipulated to devise a responsive RTI² system at your school. We end the chapter with a closer examination of the unique characteristics of special education supports and services for English learners, as well as the persistent problem of both under- and overrepresentation of these students.

Response to Instruction and Intervention (RTI²)

Although the term *response to instruction and intervention* has appeared only since 2004 in federal legislation (the Individuals with Disabilities Education Improvement Act), the practice of closely monitoring progress has existed for several decades as a practice in special education. The intent is to provide early intervention in reading and mathematics for children who might benefit from additional instruction. Response to instruction and intervention seeks to prevent the "waiting to fail" model that does a disservice to students who otherwise must demonstrate a significant skill deficit before receiving valuable supplemental instruction. It is also used as an alternative means for qualifying students with learning disabilities for special education services. These two purposes are sometimes aligned and sometimes not. Like any educational practice, RTI² can be done well, badly, or somewhere in between. When done poorly, a student is put through a perfunctory supplemental program not tailored to her unique strengths and needs, and then is rapidly qualified for special education services, where she is viewed as "someone else's problem." When done well, a responsive system of supplemental and intensive intervention, customized to meet the needs of the student, fully involves both students and their families. Special education qualification is available if and when it is needed to further the student's education.

Response to instruction and intervention is most commonly represented as a tiered approach (figure 4.1, page 46). The first tier describes a quality core program in reading and mathematics that all students receive. This is where good first teaching occurs, and it is the first place where adjustments to practice should occur in order to increase effectiveness. This is also the first place principals should look. If 70–80 percent of the students at your school are not approaching, meeting, or exceeding grade-level expectations, then the core program is in need of improvement.

Tier 2 refers to supplemental intervention. Here, the word *supplemental* is key. Instruction at this level is in addition to, not a replacement for, quality core instruction. Therefore, Tier 2 is best delivered within the child's classroom, most often by the teacher. Other personnel may be involved, but it is primarily consultative, rather than through direct services. Because of this, it is not practical to have more than 15–25 percent of the students at a school involved in supplemental interventions. These supplemental interventions often come in the form of additional small-group instruction that guides students toward greater understanding of core content.

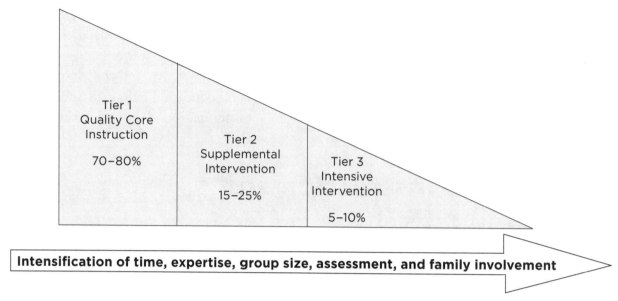

Source: Implementing RTI With English Learners, *by Douglas Fisher, Nancy Frey, and Carol Rothenberg. © 2011, Solution Tree Press. Used with permission.*

Figure 4.1. Tiers of instruction and intervention.

Tier 3 intensive intervention is reserved for students who have not demonstrated progress in Tier 2 or who are significantly delayed, as evidenced by initial screening tools. This is typically instruction that is delivered daily and individually, and is designed to increase the intensity of the intervention. By way of example, Reading Recovery is a Tier 3 intensive intervention for first-grade students. Because of the one-to-one instruction involved, other personnel are often used, and it is commonly delivered outside the grade-level classroom. The heightened degree of services limits Tier 3 services to approximately 5–10 percent of the school population. All of these percentages should be taken under advisement, as the unique nature of each school, as well as its staffing and resources, have an impact on its ability to offer a responsive intervention program.

While there is variance in the advised amount of time that should be devoted to Tier 2 and Tier 3 interventions, the general agreement is that each should last about eighteen to twenty weeks. Neither should go on indefinitely, as it is difficult to sustain this level of support for long periods. One error in designing an effective RTI[2] program is believing that the goal should be grade-level achievement. The purpose of progress monitoring is to gauge progress *toward* goals, not the *accomplishment* of goals; a primary purpose of response to intervention is to determine what works so that it can be utilized with the quality core program. And remember as well that with English learners, comparison to true peers, not just to similarly aged classmates, is in order.

The next section looks at each of the tiers in more detail.

Tier 1 Quality Core Instruction

In chapter 2, we discussed the features of quality instruction through a gradual release of responsibility framework. You will recall that these features include (Fisher & Frey, 2008):

- *Focus lessons* to establish purpose, model, and think aloud

- *Guided instruction* using robust questions, prompts, and cues

- *Collaborative learning* through productive group work

- *Independent learning* both in-class and out of school

A central assumption of effective instruction for English learners is that the teacher understands the cultural, linguistic, and experiential differences between and among his students. Gay (2000) calls this culturally responsive teaching and advises that it requires careful preparation. The research on culturally responsive teaching extends across decades (for example, Gay, 2000; Moll, Amanti, Neff, & Gonzalez, 1992; Suárez-Orozco, Suárez-Orozco, & Tordorova, 2008). And because instruction is meaningless without curriculum, in any quality core program for English learners, the curriculum is crafted to build on the collective strengths of the learners in order to expand their knowledge of the world around them.

Culturally responsive teaching includes becoming culturally aware, designing culturally relevant curriculum, building a learning community, and fostering cross-cultural communication (Gay, 2000).

- **Becoming culturally aware:** All of us are shaped by the cultural, linguistic, and experiential characteristics of our families and communities. Since we bring own cultural identities into the classroom, we must actively learn about them. This goes beyond the surface knowledge of foods and festivals (although it is a starting point). Knowledge of other cultures is built over a lifetime and may begin with learning simple greetings in another language. In time and with intention, it can deepen an understanding of gender roles, educational viewpoints, and spiritual influences.

- **Designing culturally relevant curriculum:** While state standards and frameworks guide what is taught in the classroom, the teacher can bring a unique lens to the way that material is understood. By making connections to the local context—to the lives of children and their families and the cultures they represent—students can begin to "see" themselves and others in the curriculum. Gay (2000) talks about the influence of the symbolic curriculum, especially in the materials and visual displays that children see each day in their school. The classroom itself should reflect the people who learn within it, and the books, photographs, and learning materials on display can become a rich palette for illustrating the many cultures of the community.

- **Building a learning community:** Now more than ever, making our way in the world is dependent on our ability to work with others to achieve our goals. The importance of productive group work as a chief vehicle for learning cannot be underestimated in classrooms with English learners. Not only is it vital for these students to use language in their learning, it may also be culturally consistent with their best ways of working. In many communities, the unit of analysis is the group, not the individual, and sharing and helping are valued over competition. A classroom that capitalizes on these collaborative strengths prepares students for the kind of college- and career-ready skills emphasized in the Common Core State Standards.

- **Fostering cross-cultural communication:** Traditional school discourse places the teacher at the center, with students listening and participating only when invited. This aligns with the norms of cultures in which children are expected to remain quiet and not participate unless instructed to do so. But it may clash with the values of cultures that favor a more participatory stance. A lack of understanding about this on the teacher's part may result in the confusion of communication styles with behavior issues. A major goal is to expand the registers that students are able to communicate in, including (but not limited to) classroom discourse.

Quality Indicators for Tier 1

A quality core program for English learners provides purposeful teaching and scaffolded instruction within a strength-based curriculum that builds on these students' experiences while broadening and deepening their understanding of the world. It is a tall order, but a necessary one for effective English language instruction.

- *Time* is devoted each day to mathematics and reading and language arts instruction. State and districts vary on the number of instructional minutes assigned, but typically this tier requires at least sixty minutes of math instruction and ninety minutes of literacy instruction daily.

- *Expertise* comes in the form of a highly qualified teacher who designs and implements a research-based curriculum aligned with state standards. Paraprofessionals and volunteers are used strategically to enhance the program.

- *Group size* is variable, depending on the phase of instruction. A gradual release of responsibility framework includes whole-class, small-group, and individual instruction.

- *Assessment* occurs at least three times per year in the form of benchmark assessments. These results are used to inform subsequent instruction, form groups, and identify areas of the curriculum that require reteaching.

- *Family involvement* includes providing information about the core program in a variety of forums, including Curriculum Night, teacher conferences, family math and family literacy events, and classroom newsletters. Family organizations are actively involved in these efforts, including outreach to the broader community.

Tier 2 Supplemental Intervention

When students fail to make progress with the quality core curriculum, it is necessary to offer supplemental instruction. In the language of RTI[2], this is Tier 2. The intended effect of Tier 2 is to provide a double dose of instruction in order to make Tier 1 more accessible. Therefore, Tier 2 lessons are likely to be used to build background knowledge, frontload content, and expand vocabulary knowledge. Because the purpose is to supplement, not supplant Tier 1 instruction, these lessons should be closely tied to the curriculum being taught in the quality core program. It is for this reason that separate, prepackaged Tier 2 programs are not especially useful for students who struggle. For a student who is already having difficulty with the original curriculum, introducing a second, unrelated one will result in more confusion.

In many districts, it is common to group students for English language development instruction several times a week. This type of instruction often focuses on grammar, syntax, oral language skills, and vocabulary and concept development. These temporary groups are formed across grade-level classrooms and are intended to provide targeted instruction for students at similar proficiency levels. Depending on the distribution of learners, these groups may range from just a handful to twenty or more. However, this is part of the quality core program, *not* Tier 2 supplemental intervention.

Tier 2 supplemental intervention should be delivered within the classroom in order to capitalize on the momentum established during core instruction. In practical terms, this means additional small-group instruction. The benefits of small-group instruction are significant for all learners (see Hattie, 2008, for a detailed meta-analysis), and this is especially true for students who struggle. An effective quality core program in reading and mathematics should include daily small-group instruction as a matter of form. Students identified for Tier 2 receive additional small-group instruction. While students performing at grade level meet twice a week in teacher-directed small groups, identified students meet four to five times a week.

Access to Expertise

A note of caution regarding Tier 2 supplemental intervention—expertise is key. Some schools are fortunate to have paraprofessionals and volunteers enrich the classrooms. These men and women are valuable in so many ways, especially in being able to provide students with the attention and care they deserve. However, these same people are taxed beyond the scope of their knowledge when they are asked to deliver Tier 2 intervention. Students who struggle should have access to more, not less expertise. It is the classroom teacher who is the most expert, and it is he or she who should be meeting with Tier 2 groups. The time that the teacher meets with the Tier 2 group is an ideal time for paraprofessionals and volunteers to work with the rest of the class.

Although it is the classroom teacher who is delivering instruction, the consultative support of other specialists is a welcome addition. Look at the resources you have at your school. Do you have an instructional coach? A bilingual specialist? A math or reading coach? These and other specialists can contribute valuable ideas and assessments to the ongoing conversation about supporting English learners in Tier 2. While these professionals are often eager to share with their colleagues, it can be hard for them to find the time. Creating schedules that allow for these consultative relationships to bloom should be a top priority for principals. It is amazing to witness the problem-solving capacity of groups when they are given the time and resources.

Group Size

The size of Tier 2 groups is important as well. Because the purpose of Tier 2 supplemental intervention is to build needed skills and abilities for Tier 1, these groups should be very small in size—no more than three or four English learners. That number is not arbitrary. Vaughn and Linan-Thompson (2003) examined the effects of a second-grade reading intervention and found that groups of three had a strong positive effect on learning, while larger groups of ten did not. There's good common sense involved with this as well. Supplemental intervention for English learners invariably involved oral language use, and increasing the number of students decreases the number of opportunities for interaction.

Intensified Assessment

Tier 2 supplemental intervention also requires intensification of assessment as well. In addition to the benchmark assessments of a quality core program, students in Tier 2 should be assessed at least once or twice a month to more closely monitor their progress. These assessments need not be time-consuming, but they should measure what is being taught. Therefore, timed writing or math assessments, a measure of vocabulary acquisition, or a comprehension assessment of a reading passage may be warranted. Most importantly, the results should be used to inform subsequent instruction, not simply measure skills. Without the flexibility to make midcourse corrections, teachers feel justifiably frustrated. Keep the term in mind: *response to intervention*. An overarching goal is to find what works and then use that information to benefit the learner.

Family Participation

In the rush to provide supplemental instruction, the family can be easily overlooked. This is especially true for families of English learners, who may be unfamiliar with school processes or reluctant to participate. It is vital that families feel informed and comfortable with the process, especially when their child is showing early signs of struggle. In some districts, parent liaisons may be able to offer additional assistance with or guidance in fostering family participation. It is also useful to consider meeting family members off-campus at a mutually agreed-on location. This may put the family at ease and allow them to participate more fully in the discussion. It is essential to keep in mind that these are not one-way conversations. The family often knows much more about what has been successful with their child, and their insights can be of considerable value in designing effective supplemental instruction.

Quality Indicators for Tier 2

Supplemental instruction for English learners should be tied to the quality core program and should focus on one or more broad practices, including building background knowledge, front-loading content, and expanding vocabulary and conceptual understanding. This does not mean that discrete skills must be ruled out; indeed, basic skills about phonemes, sound and letter relationships, and numeracy are critical in elementary school. However, these should not be offered in isolation from other curricular connections. Students should have the opportunity to learn and practice these skills within the context of what they are learning in the core program. Specific indicators include the following:

- *Time* is dedicated to supplemental instruction at least three times per week, and daily if possible.

- *Access to expertise* is ensured, because the teacher is the main point of contact for instruction. In turn, the teacher also has consultative access to school-based experts, including coaches, specialists, special educators, and other related services personnel. Paraprofessionals and volunteers support the other students in the class during this time.

- *Group size* is reduced to make sure that students have many opportunities to respond and participate. For this reason, the group should consist of three to four at the most. Other factors may reduce the size of the group. Younger children and those with a beginning level of language proficiency benefit from an even smaller group size.

- *Assessment* should occur once or twice a month to monitor progress and inform instruction. These assessments need not be time-consuming, but should be aligned with the instruction offered.

- *Family involvement* should occur before rather than after the fact. When concerns arise about a child's lack of progress, the family should be informed. It is important to keep in mind that information should flow both ways: remember to solicit insights and recommendations from the family.

Tier 3 Intensive Intervention

A smaller number of students need this type of intensive intervention. To use the language of the Illinois Alliance for School-Based Problem-Solving and Intervention Resources in Education (ASPIRE, 2009), while Tier 2 is about providing more support, Tier 3 is about offering the most support for students to be successful. This means intensifying time, duration, frequency, expertise, assessment, and family involvement. The goal is to ensure that the student can benefit from the quality core program, but a student does not necessarily need to be performing at grade level to do so. Keep in mind that a part of good core instruction is differentiation.

While it is not possible (or even advisable) to predict what the content of a Tier 3 intervention might look like for a given child, we can look at what the research says about this level of support for elementary students. Wanzek & Vaughn (2010) reviewed studies of Tier 3 reading interventions for elementary students and drew several conclusions.

- Kindergarten to third grade:

  › The most effective interventions combined meaningful text reading with skills instruction, especially in phonics.

  › The best results came from one-to-one instruction, with groups showing smaller gains.

  › The earlier the intervention, the better. Results in kindergarten and first grade were higher than those in second and third.

- Grades 4 and 5:

  › The most effective interventions emphasized reading comprehension and vocabulary. Fluency interventions had mixed results.

  › Multicomponent interventions that included a mix of reading comprehension instruction, vocabulary, and some fluency and phonics instruction were effective.

  › Thirty-minute one-to-one intervention models worked well when combined with the previously mentioned curricular emphases.

Mathematics Interventions

The recommendations of What Works Clearinghouse for mathematics interventions in elementary school focus on content. Five of their recommendations are identified as having a moderate or strong level of evidence to support their findings, while three have minimal evidence for effectiveness. The five with moderate or strong evidence are:

1. Screen all students to identify those at risk for potential mathematics difficulties and provide interventions to students identified as at risk. (Moderate) . . .

3. Instruction during the intervention should be explicit and systematic. This includes providing models of proficient problem solving, verbalization of thought processes, guided practice, corrective feedback, and frequent cumulative review. (*Strong*)

4. Interventions should include instruction on solving word problems that is based on common underlying structures. (*Strong*)

5. Intervention materials should include opportunities for students to work with visual representations of mathematical ideas, and interventionists should be proficient in the use of visual representations of mathematical ideas. (*Moderate*)

6. Interventions at all grade levels should devote about 10 minutes in each session to building fluent retrieval of basic arithmetic facts. (*Moderate*) (Gersten et al., 2009, p. 6)

Location, Expertise, Group Size, and Time

Because of the intensive nature of a Tier 3 intervention, it is often impractical to offer it within the classroom; it is generally provided elsewhere in the school. In addition, as in Tier 2, access to expertise is increased, and the intervention is usually delivered by someone other than the classroom teacher, such as a coach, specialist, or special education teacher. However, the limited time available to this small cadre of educators may strain the resources of the school. Our work has resulted in a favorable solution to this problem: every certificated adult without classroom responsibilities provides Tier 3 instruction to one or two students (Fisher et al., 2011). This increases our capacity to offer intensive intervention while shifting some of the workload away from the limited number of specialists in the school.

These intensive interventions are offered daily and during one-to-one instruction. Keep in mind that the name of the game at this level is "most," and it's definitely not time to hold anything back in the arsenal of good instruction. The evidence of the value of one-to-one instruction with a highly qualified teacher is strong (Frey, 2006), especially because this arrangement makes it possible to respond immediately to any difficulties or confusions the learner is experiencing.

Assessment

Individual instruction also makes it possible to assess more frequently, another hallmark of Tier 3 intervention. Progress is closely tracked and is often measured through specific skills tests called *curriculum-based measures* (CBM). These are generally fluency based and of short duration and are meant to serve as a proxy for progress in a curriculum area. Most importantly, they are normed so that a comparison can be made to expected levels of achievement. For example, the following are CBMs in reading and mathematics:

- Alphabet naming

- Timed oral fluency measure

- Math facts

- Number recognition

If this raises a note of caution, good for you! The use of curriculum-based measures with English learners *should* be approached cautiously. As a means for tracking progress over time, they can be quite effective; however, their usefulness for making eligibility decisions for special education are not as clear. When considering CBM data for this purpose, the details of the norming group are essential. Keep in mind that the progress of an English learner should be considered in relation to the progress of his or her true peers—that is, other English learners at similar proficiency levels with similar experiences in formal schooling.

Progress monitoring is also done using *curriculum-based assessments* (CBA). These are tests that use the school materials and curriculum as the basis of measurement. Although they lack the technical robustness of CBMs, curriculum-based assessments offer the advantage of a more direct link to what is being taught. For example, a student's progress through a science unit on plants is a CBA.

Family involvement at Tier 3 is crucial for the student's success. The support and encouragement a family offers can serve as a positive influence for the student. In addition, the family can reinforce what is being learned in school and share details of a students' progress. However, as we have mentioned, family involvement should not be viewed as a one-way street. Students learn both at school and at home, and a narrow view of learning only within the school context does a disservice to the student. Therefore, it is vital that educators and parents collaboratively share expertise and knowledge (Reschly, 2010).

Quality Indicators for Tier 3

Tier 3 intensive intervention is reserved for students who have failed to make progress through supplemental intervention. The goal is to elevate a student's skills so that he or she can benefit from the quality core program. Because Tier 3 results can be used for special education referral, measurements used are valid and reliable for English learners. In addition, the family's role deepens. Because RTI[2] is essentially a problem-solving process, it is essential to gain the full participation of the family. And since learning happens both at home and at school, an RTI[2] effort that leaves the family out of the equation is a diminished and less effective one. Specifically:

- *Time* in intervention is increased to daily sessions of up to thirty minutes. Younger children may need a period of time to adjust due to stamina.

- *Access to expertise* is further expanded to include specialists and coaches for direct instruction. In schools with a large number of Tier 3 students, every certificated adult (administrators, librarian, and so on) have a caseload of one or more students.

- *Group size* is decreased to individual instruction in order to maximize responsive teaching.

- *Assessments* in the form of curriculum-based measurements and curriculum-based assessments are collected and analyzed weekly to monitor progress and make instructional decisions.

- *Family involvement* is further intensified in order to ensure that parents are full members of the problem-solving team.

Table 4.1 shows a summary of the differences between Tier 1, Tier 2, and Tier 3 in terms of use of time, access to expertise, group size, assessment, and family involvement.

Under- and Overrepresentation of English Learners in Special Education

While the primary purpose of response to instruction and intervention is to provide early intervention for students in danger of falling behind, the data collected can be used as part of determining eligibility for special education supports and services. In the past, a discrepancy formula that compared expected achievement with actual achievement was used. Too often, this resulted in a significant delay of needed supports until achievement declined to a statistically significant level. This "waiting to fail" model was criticized by many educators and families who felt that precious intervention time was lost. Through the efforts of many researchers and educators, the Individuals with Disabilities Education Improvement Act of 2004 contained language that allows progress-monitoring data to be used as an alternative means of determining eligibility.

The issue of special education referrals for English learners is more complex, however. There is both an *under-* and an *over*representation of English learners in special education. Underrepresentation is apparent upon examination of the national rate: while English learners comprise 10.3 percent of the pupil population, only 5.4 percent of special education students are EL (Office of English Language Acquisition, 2008). But at the local level, rates vary widely. Louisiana, Mississippi, New Hampshire, Tennessee, and West Virginia report that less than one percent of English learners

Table 4.1. Matrix of an Effective Response to Instruction and Intervention (RTI²) Program for English Learners

	Tier 1 Quality Core Instruction	Tier 2 Supplemental Intervention	Tier 3 Intensive Intervention
Intensification of time, expertise, group size, assessment, and family involvement →			
Use of Time	Instruction is delivered daily for at least sixty minutes a day (math) and ninety minutes a day (reading and language arts).	Supplemental instruction should occur at least three times a week, in addition to the quality core program.	Intensive intervention occurs daily, for as much as thirty minutes per session.
Access to Expertise	The classroom teacher designs and delivers research-based instruction using standards-aligned curriculum.	Instruction is delivered by the classroom teacher in consultation with other school-based experts (coach, specialist).	Instruction is primarily delivered by a specialist. At schools with large numbers of Tier 3 students, all certificated personnel have a caseload.
Group Size	A mixture of whole-class, small-group, and individual instruction is offered using a gradual release of responsibility framework that includes modeling, guided instruction, collaborative learning, and independent learning.	Groups should be restricted to no more than three to four students. Age, language proficiency, and instructional purpose should also be considered when determining group size.	Instruction is one-to-one and individualized to meet the needs of the learner.
Assessment	Benchmark assessments are collected and analyzed at least three times per year. Results are used to fine tune instructional and curricular decisions.	Assessment information should be collected one to two times per month and should mirror what is being taught. The results should be used to inform subsequent instruction.	CBMs and CBAs are used carefully, so that true peers are considered. Assessment occurs weekly.
Family Involvement	Families have many outlets for understanding the quality core program, including Curriculum Night, teacher conferences, classroom newsletters, community outreach, and parent organizations.	Families are made a part of the process of identification and progress monitoring. They are informed monthly about their child's progress and subsequent instructional decisions.	Families are fully involved in the process and are seen as fellow problem solvers.

receive special education services. On the other end of the spectrum, California, Nevada, New Mexico, and Texas all report that more than 15 percent of their English learner populations are students with disabilities (Office of English Language Acquisition, 2008). Researchers have offered several explanations for this disparity (Estrada & Lavadenz, 2011; Fisher, Frey, & Rothenberg, 2011):

- A decline in first-language proficiency

- Difficulty distinguishing between language difference and disability on assessments

- Differences between home and school cultures

- Lack of bilingual special education specialists and psychologists

- Lack of diagnostic assessment tools in languages other than English

Where does your district fall? As principal of a school with English learners, it is essential that you investigate this issue at the local level. In districts and states where underrepresentation is an issue, outreach programs have been designed to identify special education referrals at an early age. For example, Child Find is funded by Part C of IDEIA to locate and serve infants and toddlers who have disabilities. While this public awareness program has been largely successful, identification is primarily confined to young children with significant cognitive, physical, and developmental disabilities. Mild disabilities such as specific learning disability and language impairment usually don't manifest themselves until school age. In order to ensure that these students are not overlooked, some districts are actively recruiting specialists trained in English learner issues to be members of RTI² and student study teams.

Overrepresentation of English learners plagues other systems. While psychometric issues for discerning between language difference and language disability exist, progress is being made. As RTI² efforts become more widespread, a research base of best practices is emerging regarding instruction, intervention, and assessment for English learners (Linan-Thompson, Cirino, & Vaughn, 2007). Ongoing professional development about issues related to language development, supporting English learners, and disproportionality can raise awareness among teachers. Similar parent education efforts should be made for families in your community as well.

Conclusion

While not all English learners will require supplemental and intensive interventions, some will. As a leader, you will be tasked with determining which students need additional support to accelerate their learning and ensure their success. You will likely have to develop, implement, and monitor these intervention efforts and recruit staff members to support the effort. In focusing your attention on the intervention needs of English learners, you'll want to keep in mind the components of an effective response to instruction and intervention effort:

- Quality core instruction

- Screening

- Early intervention using evidence-based instruction

- Progress monitoring

- Data-based decision making

When intervention is aligned with instruction and assessment, English learners' progress is noticed, monitored, and improved. As the instructional leader, your role is to ensure that English learners are supported as they become contributing members of the school and community.

Fostering a Quality Program for English Learners

Education in general is fraught with controversy: How should children be taught? Toward what end? By whom, and for how long? Discussion about the education of students learning to speak English can be especially heated. The debate can drift from effective classroom practice to rhetoric about national identity, culture and tradition, and even what the founders of this country intended over two hundred years ago. Caught in the middle of this swirl are children who possess widely different skills, strengths, and areas of need. As educators, we are charged with shepherding them into a future that, given the rapid pace of change we have witnessed in the last fifty years, will be quite different from the world we live in now.

What We Know and Don't Yet Know

Big Idea

A quality program for English learners is developed and improved only with the participation of stakeholders. These include educators and personnel at the school, students and their families, and middle schools that your students will attend in the future. There is much to be learned from these stakeholders as research continues to shape policy and practice.

Questions Principals Ask

- What is known, and not yet known, about instruction for English learners?
- How can I cultivate teacher expertise about English learners at my school?
- In what ways can I promote collaboration with families?
- How can I support preparation of students for middle school?
- How can I become a more informed principal?

We would never suggest that we know everything about what is "best" for educating English learners. To the contrary, we are as plagued as you are about what constitutes effective and honorable practice. And perhaps that is the most important takeaway in this book: while we know more about children's education than we knew ten years ago, there is still much to learn. Claude Goldenberg (2008) summarized two major works about English learners—the National Literacy Panel meta-analysis (August & Shanahan, 2006) and the review of the Center for Research on

Education, Diversity, and Excellence (Genesee, Lindholm-Leary, Saunders, & Christian, 2006). He posed three questions that still lack a clear answer:

- Bilingual reading instruction helps, but in what settings? With which students? For how long?

- Can ELLs' oral English development be accelerated? How?

- What is the best way to teach English language development? (Goldenberg, 2008, pp. 12–13)

These questions are often at the center of debate on how best to support English learners, and while research on these vital issues continues to emerge, the weight of the evidence is not yet sufficient to make clear-cut decisions on all points. However, policies cannot be held in abeyance while we stand by waiting for all the research. As a principal, you are held accountable for guiding your school according to the local and state policies that have been created. These policies have changed and will continue to do so. Like the knowledge base, they are not static. This can be bewildering and frustrating for stakeholders, who may interpret these changes as capricious or even sinister. As a meaning maker for the district, it is necessary to know the difference between what is known, what is believed, and what is not yet known.

And it's not all bad news—the field knows a lot about what does work. We turn again to Goldenberg's (2008) summary of the research on English learners:

- Teaching students to read in their first language promotes higher levels of reading achievement in English;

- What we know about good instruction and curriculum in general holds true for English learners as well; but

- When instructing English learners in English, teachers must modify instruction to take into account students' language limitations. (p. 14)

Local and state policies definitely come into play on these matters as well, especially regarding the first point. Depending on laws and regulations where you live, instruction in a student's first language may not be possible. The unique demographics of your local area might also make this impractical, especially if your classrooms are composed of students who speak a variety of languages. While 80 percent of English learners speak Spanish, the other 20 percent represent four hundred additional languages (Goldenberg, 2008)! There may not be qualified adults available to teach these students in their primary language.

What Works

No one person can be the keeper of all the knowledge of what is best for teaching English learners. We need to involve all the stakeholders in order to enrich the discussion on what works and find practical solutions for implementation. It's a mutually beneficial relationship: as we build the capacity of the people we work with and for, they help increase what *we* know as well. These stakeholders include the educators that work inside and out of the classrooms at your school, the families of your students, and the middle schools your students will attend in the future. In the following section, we add to Goldenberg's list what we know also works and then discuss each point at greater length in the remainder of this chapter:

- Invest in teacher development around issues of language and diversity at every phase of educators' careers.

- Collaborate with families and the community to improve student learning.

- Engage with middle schools to more fully prepare English learners for the next phase of schooling.

Invest in Teacher Development

As a principal, you are tasked with being the instructional leader of your school. And while the details of curriculum at all grade levels may be beyond the scope of your expertise, understanding the fundamentals of sound instruction and curriculum is not. Messages about instruction and curriculum stem from several sources, including content standards, district initiatives, and the collective wisdom of the teaching staff in the building. The principal must bring these threads together to articulate a coherent message about the school's practices. This is perhaps best seen in the development of teachers across their careers. When there is a consistent and coherent message about effective practices, teachers have time to integrate them into their repertoire, but if the expectations change regularly, teachers do not feel that they become proficient in any one practice. Berliner (1994) described five stages of expertise in teaching, noting that not everyone will rise to the level of expert in the course of his or her career. This might be elaborated as follows:

> *Stage 1: Novice level—"The deliberate learner."* Minimal skills driven by context-free rules ("Praise when a student gives the right answer") as seen in student teachers and some first-year teachers.
>
> *Stage 2: Advanced beginner level—"The insightful learner."* Draws upon past experience to inform decisions but does not accept full personal agency for outcomes, as seen in second-year teachers.
>
> *Stage 3: Competent level—"The rational learner."* Sets goals, makes plans, and accepts responsibility but is not yet fluid or fluent. Third- and fourth-year teachers may reach this level, and some teachers never move beyond this stage of expertise.
>
> *Stage 4: Proficient level—"The intuitive learner."* Some teachers reach the stage of being able to teach analytically and intuitively, drawing on both past experience and a deep knowledge base.
>
> *Stage 5: Expert level—"The arational learner."* Teaches fluently and seemingly effortlessly but may have more difficulty in putting instructional decisions into words. Solutions to problems are creative and intuitive. (Frey & Fisher, 2009, p. 400)

Now consider teacher expertise through the lens of our knowledge base about English learners. What do the teachers at your school know and understand about language and diversity? A proficient teacher of mathematics may be only at the advanced beginner stage when it comes to understanding English learner issues. Induction, professional development, mentoring, and coaching all play an important role in increasing the expertise of your staff.

As with other aspects of instruction and curriculum, knowledge about English learners needs to be purposefully cultivated. In too many cases, we have seen it added on as an afterthought, usually lumped in with special education issues, which also deserve more attention than they typically receive. The attitude of "Oh yeah, _____ is good for English learners and students with disabilities, too" not only gives short shrift to these students, but also sends an unintended message to teachers that neither population is of particular importance. As noted in numerous research findings, what constitutes good instruction in general is also good English learner instruction (for example, August & Shanahan, 2006; Brown & Doolittle, 2008; Genesee et al., 2006; Gersten et al., 2009). By placing English learners at the center of professional development, other students will benefit as well. A way of considering the relative expertise of teachers at your school on the topic of language learners is to use Berliner's stage model, modified by us to describe teachers' knowledge bases and practices. These include:

Stage 1—Knowledge of the context for English learners

Stage 2—Knowledge of the pedagogy of language development

Stage 3—Knowledge of accurate and culturally sensitive assessment practices

Stage 4—Knowledge of specialized intervention for English learners who struggle

Stage 5—Knowledge of adult collaboration and communication across professional and family communities

Table 5.1 contains a more detailed list.

This affects staffing decisions as well. To put it bluntly, classrooms with English learners need and deserve the most expert teachers on your staff. Unfortunately, in some schools the most inexperienced teachers are assigned to the most challenging classes. This contributes heavily to the high attrition rate among beginning teachers. In fact, an appalling 9.1 percent of teachers in their first three years left teaching in the year 2008–09, and an additional 13.7 percent moved to another school (U.S. Department of Education, 2010). We simply can't afford this kind of turnover on the staffs of diversity-rich schools.

Whether helping new teachers feel supported in their professional growth or fostering increasing levels of expertise among more experienced staff, sophisticated professional development is key. Bruce Joyce and Beverly Showers (2002) recommend a multidimensional approach to cultivating teacher knowledge through professional development. Their model includes:

- Professional development events about curriculum, instruction, and the learning climate

- Coaching and mentoring for application in the classroom

- Ongoing evaluation of professional development, including data-driven decision making based on student outcomes

- Inquiry-based planning to identify next steps for focused professional development

Table 5.1. Keys to Professional Development for Teachers of English Learners

Domain	Key Practices
Stage 1: Contextual Knowledge	Becoming aware of students and the context in which they live
	Developing achievement and proficiency profiles of students
	Supporting English learners with programmatic features
	Becoming familiar with cultural norms and traditions
Stage 2: Pedagogical Knowledge	Integrating language development into content
	Capitalizing on first-language strengths to build proficiency
	Accommodating language proficiency in daily teaching
	Promoting competence of students within the school community
	Building community in the classroom
	Fostering connections between home and school
Stage 3: Assessment Knowledge	Developing assessment practices for determining proficiency
	Utilizing informative assessments in daily teaching
	Creating and implementing testing accommodations based on language proficiency
	Utilizing assessment information to improve teaching and learning
	Collaborating with families regarding assessment decisions and problem solving
Stage 4: Intervention Knowledge	Ensuring early identification of students who may benefit from intervention
	Using progress-monitoring and diagnostic tools with targeted students
	Understanding the role of true peers in interpreting data
	Organizing collaborative partnerships among school educators, parent educators, and specialists
	Leading innovative family literacy and family numeracy programs
Stage 5: Expert Knowledge	Informing other stakeholders about English learner issues
	Coaching and mentoring other educators to increase their expertise
	Seeking knowledge of current research about language development
	Leading efforts to create more "homelike" schools that capitalize on family practices of teaching and learning

A multidimensional professional development system requires that teacher expertise be cultivated using all of these tools. A ninety-minute presentation about English learners in an after-school professional development session may spark conversation, but it is insufficient to influence classroom practice. The coaching and mentoring of teachers by administrators and teacher-leaders must be purposeful if change is to be seen. The principal's commitment to ongoing professional development is paramount.

Collaborate With Families and the Community

While we have come a long way since the day in 1930 when the principal at Lemon Grove Grammar School barred the schoolhouse door to Mexican parents and their children, our schools are not always as welcoming as we would like to believe they are. Researchers have documented the ambivalent feelings of families who avoid the school campus due to differences in culture, language, communication, and values (Lapp, Fisher, Flood, & Moore, 2002; Lee, 2005; Valdés, 1996). Lee's analysis of the selective participation of Korean families at their children's elementary school found the following impediments:

- *Language barriers* that made it difficult for families with limited English skills to understand school processes and to make their ideas understood to school personnel

- *Time barriers* that did not allow families to participate (most meetings were scheduled in the middle of the day, requiring some families to close down their businesses in order to be at school)

- *Written communication* in the form of newsletters and announcements, not provided in languages other than English

- *Cultural norms about authority* that made it difficult for parents to challenge decisions, even when they disagreed

- *Cultural differences regarding the amount of time parents should spend in school* caused passive misunderstandings. One parent in the study said, "In Korea we don't usually go to our children's school and stay there for so many hours. . . . If you show up at the school often or on a regular basis to see the teacher or you're just there too much, you're sure to end up in a string of rumors that you're trying to bribe the teacher or ask that your child be treated in a special way" (Lee, 2005, p. 306).

Although this study focused on the perceptions of Korean families, families from other language and cultural backgrounds have similar concerns. Fortunately, many of these barriers can be eliminated through thoughtful planning that keeps the needs of families at the center of the discussion. For example, many districts have parent educators and family involvement initiatives that can provide schools with assistance and resources for supporting families of English learners. Most schools have a parent organization that raises funds, gathers information, and advises the administrator. If it has not already occurred on your campus, expand the scope of this organization beyond its traditional bounds to become a full-fledged parent center for the community.

Other practices are mandated to prevent the kind of alienation that keeps families disengaged from the school. The May 25 (1970) Memorandum from the U.S. Department of Health, Education and Welfare states that "school districts have the responsibility to adequately notify national origin-minority group parents of school activities which are called to the attention of other parents. Such notice in order to be adequate may have to be provided in a language other than English" (U.S. Department of Health, Education, and Welfare, 1970). Today forms are routinely available in other languages (although it is less common to see newsletters and other forms of information translated). When sending home information to families, consult with your school's parent center and the district's English Learner Department to find out how translation services can be accessed.

These practices are the minimal steps required to create a welcoming environment. But our schools need more than the minimum. In order to better serve students who are learning English, we must find more sophisticated ways to support them. If we acknowledge that learning happens first at home and continues throughout the child's school years, then it is necessary for us to improve the ways we can capitalize on this. Traditional family literacy and numeracy programs have sought to infuse school practices into the home, with limited success. But think about what we know about learning. We know that a transmission model of teaching where students are regarded as empty vessels to pour knowledge into is simply not effective. Why would we expect families to respond any differently? The emphasis on making homes more like an extension of school is shortsighted. We should be actively finding ways to make our schools more like home (Frey, 2010).

Consider the characteristics of a resilient family system: there is affection and appreciation for one another, a shared sense of commitment to common goals, positive communication among its members, the ability to cope with a crisis, and time spent together (Stinnett & DeFrain, 1985). Aren't these the same qualities we strive for in school? A truly collaborative partnership between families and the school would seek to create similar conditions with the community. At a school where families are appreciated, the rich cultural diversity of its students is celebrated. A sense of commitment toward goals comes from groups creating them together, instead of having one group simply inform the other. Positive communication in such a community means not only communication in the family's primary language, but also making sure that they hear about the wonderful things their child is doing. In too many cases, families don't hear from the school until a problem arises. Finally, time in each other's company must be sought out. Although both teachers and families are busy, finding ways to enjoy each other's company is an incredible investment. As an example, we worked with an elementary school that began hosting monthly spaghetti dinners for all the kindergarten students. There wasn't any agenda—people simply gathered to share a meal and enjoy each other's company. Rarely have we ever witnessed a more valuable investment than those dinners.

You don't have to host a series of spaghetti dinners to bond with families. In fact, you probably have much more creative ideas. But the decision to incorporate the best qualities of home into the school can be the start of an amazing partnership. And as with any family system, we experience a mixture of pride and sadness as our children grow and move on to new chapters in their lives. For the elementary principal, this transition happens as students depart for the middle school.

Prepare Students for Middle School

Only educators view schooling in compartmentalized structures; students and families experience K–12 schooling as a much more fluid process. They expect us to know a great deal about what is expected of their children beyond the elementary school, and they rightly expect that we will adequately prepare them for it. One of the stakeholder groups, important for all students but critical to the success of English learners, is the middle school staff. As the leader, it's part of your responsibility to develop and implement transition plans to ensure that students are well prepared for their early adolescent learning experiences. If you ask students the questions they have about going to middle school, you're likely to hear:

- "Will they tease me?"

- "Will I be able to find my classes?"

- "How will I remember all of my teachers?"

- "What if I can't find the bathroom in that big school?"

- "Will there be a lot of homework?"

One of the easiest ways to alleviate the basic concerns that all students have about the transition to middle school is to organize a tour. Provide students with an opportunity to visit a middle school, find the bathroom and office, and see the classrooms and students. These future middle school students will be more comfortable once they know their way around the building. If at all possible, arrange to have current middle school students guide your elementary school students during their visit. When students serve as ambassadors for their school, they will also work to end bullying, one of the common occurrences in middle schools (Frey & Fisher, 2008).

While tours are effective, even more can be done to ensure a smooth transition to middle school. In preparation for the tour, you can invite former elementary school students now in middle school to visit your school's classrooms and answer questions. In addition, hold parent informational sessions, and explain to parents that their children are often afraid of middle school and that the family should discuss, with pride, the increasing responsibility that this transition entails. Following are five recommendations of the National Middle School Association (n.d.) for parents whose children are in transition to middle school:

1. Encourage parents to buy a combination lock before school and have their child spend time trying to open the lock. Call the school to see if they will allow him or her to practice. If you don't have the combination, make one up.

2. Go to the school two or three days before school starts, and get a copy of your child's schedule. Then take a few minutes to walk from room to room with your child. Look for direct routes to classrooms, stop by the gym, check out the locker rooms, and spend a few minutes in the lunchroom. This will help alleviate apprehensions your child and you might have about going to the middle school.

3. Don't buy backpacks that can store 50 pounds of materials. Remember, the students are not going to hike a mountain or spend two weeks in the wilderness. Keep backpacks simple. They should be able to hold a few items. The more the backpack can hold, the more a middle school student will place in it. Smaller backpacks allow for better organization.

4. Increase your knowledge of adolescent development. Take time to review information and materials that relate to middle level issues.

5. If you have raised adolescents, be willing to share advice and information with other parents. Form an information group or support group for parents of new middle school students. Also, ask the principal if they would like some volunteers for the first few days to help students with their schedules and lockers.

Another powerful way to ensure that students are prepared for middle school is for teachers to hold and communicate realistic expectations for those years. Teachers who say, "Just wait until you get to middle school to see how much work you have to do" make it sound scary and threatening.

This is a great topic for faculty development, as many teachers may not be aware that they are telegraphing negative messages about middle schools. As their principal, you should bring this to their attention and challenge assumptions teachers may have about middle school experiences.

It is vital that the receiving faculty have information about English learners who are making the transition from elementary school to middle school—specifically, information related to language proficiency and the types of support that have worked for that student in the past. In many school districts, teachers or an English learner program coordinator create a summary worksheet so that the middle school staff have information right away about the student, in case the student files take some time in arriving at the school. A sample Student Profile Form can be found on page 66.

An Ending and a Beginning

Much of this chapter has been about continuous improvement. We have discussed the importance of multifaceted professional development as a means for increasing teacher expertise about English learners. In addition, we have called for a deepening of the relationship we have with families of all students, especially those who are learning English. And finally, we have discussed ways to actively partner with middle schools to smooth the transition for these students. A final aspect of continuous improvement shouldn't be overlooked: your own. Principals are often expected to be providers of information, but it is essential for them to renew their own fund of knowledge as well.

Our final resource can be found in the Principal's Self-Study and Reflection Guide (page 67). It contains questions designed to prompt your thinking and encourage conversation with various stakeholders about the current status of your school. It can be overwhelming to think about all of the possible issues you might need to address regarding English learners. We hope this guide assists you in considering and prioritizing initiatives. Although the complexities of teaching English learners can be daunting, it is well worth the investment. So many of the children and families in our schools have endured hardships in order to make a better life. Education is essential. We're grateful that committed educators like you are making that possible every day.

Student Profile Form

Student name: _____ Grade: _____ Age: _____

Date: _____ Current Proficiency Level: _____

Previous Year Proficiency Level: _____

Areas of strength and interest: _____

_____

_____

Successful instructional approaches (Tier 1): _____

_____

_____

Participation in specialized instruction or intervention (Tier 2 or Tier 3): _____

_____

_____

Communication strengths and needs (reading, writing, speaking, and listening): _____

_____

_____

Grading and assessment accommodations: _____

_____

_____

Important family and health information: _____

_____

_____

Principal's Self-Study and Reflection Guide

School: _____ Date: _____

Principal: _____

English Learner Coordinator: _____

What is the process for identifying English learners at your school? Who is responsible for home language surveys, assessments, parent notification, and so on?	
Are English learners purposefully placed in classes according to their proficiency levels and instructional needs? Who determines class placement and monitors transferring students during the year? How is this communicated to families?	
Are English learners taught by appropriately credentialed teachers? Are these teachers engaged in continuous professional development?	
Are students acquiring English according to expectations? Who is responsible for progress monitoring? How often is this done? How is this communicated to families?	
Are English learners receiving access to grade-level core curriculum with specialized instruction and primary language support?	
Are all students who require interventions receiving those interventions? From whom? When? Is the system of intervention effective? How is this communicated with families?	
What is the process for reclassifying English learners? Is there follow-up for at least two years beyond reclassification? What happens when follow-up reveals a student who is experiencing difficulty? How is this communicated to families?	
How do you evaluate the overall effectiveness of the English learner program? Are English learners making timely progress in English acquisition and attainment of grade-level standards?	
What professional development activities are provided for teachers to build and maintain the skills and knowledge they need in order to provide high-quality instruction and intervention for English learners?	

A PRINCIPAL'S GLOSSARY

basic interpersonal communication skills (BICS). Term used to describe the social and non-academic communication used in everyday speech.

benchmark assessments. Longer assessments administered at regular intervals throughout the school year to provide the teacher and administrator with formative assessment information to inform teaching.

code-switching. The mixture of two languages used concurrently in speech, as when a person uses both English and Spanish in a conversation.

cognitive academic language proficiency (CALP). Mastery of classroom and content discourse used to discuss abstract concepts and ideas.

cognitive load. The amount of information the working memory must handle. English learners often have a higher cognitive load than monolingual students due to increased processing between two languages.

common assessments. Teacher-developed assessments whose results are discussed collaboratively to form hypotheses about the relationship between teaching and learning and to fine-tune instructional practice.

consensus scoring. The practice of examining student work with other teachers for the purpose of calibrating scoring criteria. This is especially valuable for holistic scoring, as when scoring a writing assessment.

curriculum-based assessments (CBA). Tools that use a school's materials and curriculum as the basis of measurement, offering the advantage of a more direct link to what is being taught.

curriculum-based measurements (CBM). Tools that assess students' basic academic proficiency such as math, reading, writing, and spelling.

English as a second language (ESL). A program descriptor more commonly used in secondary education, in which students receive content instruction using approaches designed for English learners.

English learner (EL). A student who speaks, and perhaps reads and writes, in a primary language that is not English and who is usually limited English proficient (LEP); also called an English language learner (ELL).

English only. Usually, a monolingual English speaker.

formative assessments. A collective term referring to the set of instructional practices teachers use to check for understanding and make decisions about what should be taught next, and to whom.

generation 1.5. Students born in the United States or who arrived at an early age.

home language. The first language learned by the child; the language used in the home.

initially fluent English proficient (IFEP). A student who speaks languages in addition to English, with initial evidence of proficiency in English.

L_1. A person's first language.

L_2. A person's second language.

language objective. Support for English learners that involves professional development, feedback, and clear expectations.

limited English proficiency (LEP). A federal designation used to describe students who do not possess enough English to reach expected standards. Because it suggests a deficit, this term is increasingly being replaced with English learner or English language learner.

newcomer. A student, traditionally in grade 3 or higher, who is new to English; a recent arrival to the United States who has limited formal schooling and may perform significantly below grade level.

progress monitoring. A collective term used to describe formative assessment tools and practices that are designed to inform teaching. Progress monitoring is an important aspect of response to intervention practices.

quality core instruction. In an RTI or RTI[2] model, the instruction that all students receive. This instruction should be based on research evidence and should result in significant numbers of students experiencing success.

realia. Real objects, as opposed to photographs or symbols that are used in instruction to demonstrate a concept or idea.

redesignated fluent English proficient (RFEP). Students who have been previously identified as English learners and have met some exit criteria, usually including a formal measure of English proficiency.

RTI[2]. Response to instruction and intervention, the practice of closely monitoring progress in order to provide early intervention where needed; an alternative to the "waiting to fail" model, according to which students must demonstrate a significant skill deficit before receiving valuable supplemental instruction. The term first appeared in the Individuals with Disabilities Education Improvement Act of 2004.

screening tools. Brief assessments that provide a snapshot of a learner's developmental, language, or cognitive abilities for the purpose of identifying children who should be further assessed for possible early intervention.

sheltered instruction observation protocol (SIOP). A commercial professional development program for using the SDAIE approach.

specially designed academic instruction in English (SDAIE). An approach to instruction for English learners that includes attention to scaffolded instruction using verbal and visual supports, carefully paced lessons, collaborative learning with peers, and frequent checks for understanding.

supplemental instruction. Lessons closely tied to the curriculum that build background knowledge, frontload content, and expand vocabulary knowledge to help students reach Tier 1.

total physical response (TPR). An approach used with newcomers to English that relies on movement, gestures, facial expressions, and demonstration to facilitate new language acquisition.

true peers. Students who, in addition to being similarly aged, share similar language proficiencies, culture, and experiential backgrounds.

REFERENCES

Abedi, J., Lord, C., & Plummer, J. (1997). *Language background as a variable in NAEP mathematics performance* (CSE Technical Report 429). Los Angeles: University of California, National Center for Research on Evaluation, Standards, and Student Testing.

Alvarez, R., Jr. (1986). The Lemon Grove incident: The nation's first successful desegregation case. *San Diego Historical Society Quarterly, 32*(2). Accessed at www.sandiegohistory.org/journal/86spring /lemongrove.htm on August 22, 2011.

Asher, J. J. (1969). The total physical response approach to second language learning. *Modern Language Journal, 53*(1), 3–17.

August, D., & Shanahan, T. (Eds.). (2006). *Developing literacy in second-language learners: Report of the national literacy panel on language-minority children and youth.* Mahwah, NJ: Erlbaum.

Bailey, A. L., & Kelly, K. R. (2010). *The use and validity of home language surveys in state English language proficiency assessment systems: A review and issues perspective.* Accessed at www.eveaproject .com/doc/HLS%20White%20Paper%202010.pdf on August 22, 2011.

Ballantyne, K. G., Sanderman, A. R., & Levy, J. (2008). *Educating English language learners: Building teacher capacity.* Washington, DC: National Clearinghouse for English Language Acquisition. Accessed at www.ncela.gwu.edu/files/uploads/3/EducatingELLsBuildingTeacherCapacityVol1 .pdf on August 23, 2011.

Beavers, J. (1999). *Developmental reading assessment.* Parsippany, NJ: Celebration Press.

Berliner, D. C. (1994). Expertise: The wonder of exemplary performance. In J. N. Mangieri & C. C. Block (Eds.), *Creating powerful thinking in teachers and students: Diverse perspectives* (pp. 161–186). Fort Worth, TX: Harcourt Brace College.

Brown v. the Board of Education, 347 U.S. 483. (1954).

Brown, J. E., & Doolittle, J. (2008). *A cultural, linguistic, and ecological framework for response to intervention with English language learners.* Tempe, AZ: National Center for Culturally Responsive Educational Systems.

Capps, R., Fix, M. E., Murray, J., Ost, J., Passel, J. S., & Hernandez, S. H. (2005). *The new demography of America's schools: Immigration and the No Child Left Behind Act.* Washington, DC: The Urban Institute.

Castañada v. Pickard, 648 F. 2d 989 (5th Cir. 1981).

Cummins, J. (1982). *Bilingualism and minority-language children.* Toronto: Ontario Institute for Studies in Education.

DuFour, R., DuFour, R., & Eaker, R. (2008). *Revisiting professional learning communities at work: New insights for improving schools.* Bloomington, IN: Solution Tree Press.

Dutro, S., & Moran, C. (2003). *Rethinking English language instruction: An architectural approach.* Newark, DE: International Reading Association.

Echevarria, J., Short, D., & Powers, K. (2006). School reform and standards-based education: A model for English-language learners. *Journal of Educational Research, 99*(4), 195–210.

Echevarria, J., Vogt, M. J., & Short, D. (2010). *Making content comprehensible for elementary English learners: The SIOP model.* Boston: Allyn & Bacon.

Estrada, K., & Lavadenz, M. (2011). Factors influencing the disproportionality of ELs with specific learning disability. *AccELLerate, 3*(3), 23.

Fisher, D., & Frey, N. (2007a). *Checking for understanding: Formative assessment techniques for your classroom.* Alexandria, VA: Association for Supervision and Curriculum Development.

Fisher, D., & Frey, N. (2007b). Implementing a schoolwide literacy framework: Improving achievement in an urban elementary school. *The Reading Teacher, 61,* 32–43.

Fisher, D., & Frey, N. (2008). *Better learning through structured teaching: A framework for the gradual release of responsibility.* Alexandria, VA: Association for Supervision and Curriculum Development.

Fisher, D., & Frey, N. (2010a). *Guided instruction: How to develop confident and successful learners.* Alexandria, VA: Association for Supervision and Curriculum Development.

Fisher, D., & Frey, N. (2010b). Unpacking the language purpose: Vocabulary, structure, and function. *TESOL Journal, 1*(3), 315–337.

Fisher, D., & Frey, N., & Rothenberg, C. (2008). *Content-area conversations: How to plan discussion-based lessons for diverse language learners.* Alexandria, VA: Association for Supervision and Curriculum Development.

Fisher, D., Frey, N., & Rothenberg, C. (2011). *Implementing RTI with English learners.* Bloomington, IN: Solution Tree Press.

Fisher, D., Rothenberg, C., & Frey, N. (2007). *Language learners in the English classroom.* Urbana, IL: National Council of Teachers of English.

Francis, D., Rivera, M., Lesaux, N., Kieffer, M., & Rivera, H. (2006). *Practical guidelines for the education of English language learners: Research-based recommendations for the use of accommodations in large-scale assessments.* Portsmouth, NH: RMC Research, Center on Instruction. Accessed at www.centeroninstruction.org/files/ELL3-Assessments.pdf on August 22, 2011.

Frey, N. (2006). The role of 1:1 individual instruction in reading. *Theory Into Practice, 45*(3), 207–214.

Frey, N. (2010). Home is not where you live, but where they understand you. In K. Dunsmore & D. Fisher (Eds.), *Bringing literacy home* (pp. 42–52). Newark, DE: International Reading Association.

Frey, N., & Fisher, D. (2007). *Reading for information in elementary school: Content literacy strategies to build comprehension.* Upper Saddle River, NJ: Pearson Merrill/Prentice Hall.

Frey, N., & Fisher, D. (2008). The under-appreciated role of humiliation in the middle school. *Middle School Journal, 39*(5), 4–13.

Frey, N., & Fisher, D. (2009). Protecting our investment: Induction and mentoring of novice teachers in diversity-rich schools. In L. M. Morrow, R. Rueda, & D. Lapp (Eds.), *Handbook of research on literacy and diversity* (pp. 396–412). New York: Guilford Press.

Frey, N., Fisher, D., & Everlove, S. (2009). *Productive group work: How to engage students, build teamwork, and promote understanding.* Alexandria, VA: Association for Supervision and Curriculum Development.

Gay, G. (2000). *Culturally responsive teaching: Theory, research, and practice.* New York: Teachers College Press.

Genesee, F., Lindholm-Leary, K., Saunders, W., & Christian, D. (2006). *Educating English language learners.* New York: Cambridge University Press.

Gersten, R., Beckmann, S., Clarke, B., Foegen, A., Marsh, L., Star, J. R., et al. (2009). *Assisting students struggling with mathematics: Response to Intervention (RtI) for elementary and middle schools* (NCEE 2009–4060). Washington, DC: National Center for Education Evaluation and Regional Assistance, Institute of Education Sciences, U.S. Department of Education. Accessed at http://ies. ed.gov/ncee/wwc/publications/practiceguides/ on August 22, 2011.

Goldenberg, C. (2008). Teaching English language learners: What the research does—and does not—say. *American Educator, 32*(2), 8–23, 42–44.

Halliday, M. A. K. (1975). *Learning how to mean: Explorations in the development of language.* New York: Arnold.

Hattie, J. (2008). *Visible learning: A synthesis of over 800 meta-analyses relating to achievement.* New York: Routledge.

Hill, J., & Flynn, K. (2006). *Classroom instruction that works with English language learners.* Alexandria, VA: Association for Supervision and Curriculum Development.

Illinois ASPIRE. (2009). *Reading and response to intervention (RtI): Putting it all together.* Accessed at www .illinoisaspire.org/welcome/files/Reading_RtI_Guide.pdf on August 22, 2011.

Individuals With Disabilities Education Improvement Act, 20 U.S.C. § 1400 (2004).

Johnson, E., Mellard, D. F., Fuchs, D., & McKnight, M. A. (2006). *Responsiveness to intervention (RTI): How to do it.* Lawrence, KS: National Research Center on Learning Disabilities.

Joyce, B., & Showers, B. (2002). *Student achievement through staff development* (3rd ed.). Alexandria, VA: Association for Supervision and Curriculum Development.

Krashen, S. D. (1982). *Principles and practice in second language acquisition.* Oxford, UK: Pergamon Press.

La Celle-Peterson, M. W., & Rivera, C. (1994). Is it real for all kids? A framework for equitable assessment policies for English language learners. *Harvard Educational Review, 64*(1), 55–75.

Lapp, D., Fisher, D., Flood, J., & Moore, K. (2002). "I don't want to teach it wrong": An investigation of the role families believe they should play in the early literacy development of their children. In D. L. Schallert, C. M. Fairbanks, J. Worthy, B. Maloch, & J. V. Hoffman (Eds.), *51st yearbook of the National Reading Conference* (pp. 275–287). Oak Creek, WI: National Reading Conference.

Lau v. Nichols, 414 U.S. 563. (1974).

Lee, S. (2005). Selective parent participation: Structural and cultural factors that influence school participation among Korean parents. *Equity and Excellence in Education, 38*(4), 299–308.

Linan-Thompson, S., Cirino, P. T., & Vaughn, S. (2007). Determining English language learners' response to intervention: Questions and some answers. *Learning Disability Quarterly, 30*(3), 185–195.

Moll, L. C., Amanti, C., Neff, D., & Gonzalez, N. (1992). Funds of knowledge for teaching: Using a qualitative approach to connect homes and classrooms. *Theory into Practice, 31*(1), 132–141.

National Clearinghouse for English Language Acquisition & Language Instruction Educational Programs (NCELA). (2011). *The growing numbers of limited English proficient students 1998/9–2008/9.* Accessed at www.ncela.gwu.edu/files/uploads/9/growingLEP_0809.pdf on August 22, 2011.

National Middle School Association. (n.d.). *The elementary to middle school transition: Five helpful hints for parents.* Accessed at www.nmsa.org/publications/webexclusive/helpfulhints/tabid/649/default.aspx on October 21, 2011

No Child Left Behind Act of 2001, 20 U.S.C. § 6319 (2008).

Office of English Language Acquisition, Language Enhancement, and Academic Achievement for Limited English Proficient Students. (2008). *Biennial report to Congress on the implementation of the Title III State Formula Grant Program: School years 2004–06.* Washington, DC: U.S. Department of Education.

Pearson, P. D., & Gallagher, G. (1983). The gradual release of responsibility model of instruction. *Contemporary Educational Psychology, 8*, 112–123.

Peregoy, S. F., & Boyle, O. F. (1997). Reading, writing, and learning in ESL. New York: Longman.

Quintanar-Sarellana, R. (2004). ¡Si se puede! Academic excellence and bilingual competency in a K–8 two-way dual immersion program. *Journal of Latinos and Education, 3*(2), 87–102.

Ragan, A., & Lesaux, N. (2006). Federal, state, and district level English language learner program entry and exit requirements: Effects on the education of language minority learners. *Education Policy Analysis Archives, 14*(20). Accessed at http://epaa.asu.edu/epaa/v14n20/ on August 22, 2011.

Ramirez, J. D., & Merino, B. (1990). Classroom talk in English immersion, early-exit and late-exit transitional bilingual education programs. In R. Jacobson & C. J. Faltis (Eds.), *Language distribution issues in bilingual schools* (pp. 61–103). Bristol, PA: Multilingual Matters.

Reschly, A. L. (2010). *Schools, families, and response to intervention.* Accessed at www.rtinetwork.org /essential/family/schools-familes-and-rti on August 22, 2011.

Rivera, C., Collum, E., Willner, L. S., & Sia, J. K., Jr. (2006). An analysis of state assessment policies regarding the accommodation of English language learners. In C. Rivera & E. Collum (Eds.), *State assessment policy and practice for English language learners: A national perspective* (pp. 1–173). Mahwah, NJ: Erlbaum.

Rothenberg, C., & Fisher, D. (2007). *Teaching English language learners: A differentiated approach.* Upper Saddle River, NJ: Merrill/Prentice Hall.

Short, D. J., & Boyson, B. A. (2004). *Creating access: Language and academic programs for secondary school newcomers.* McHenry, IL: Delta Systems.

Short, D. J., & Fitzsimmons, S. (2007). *Double the work: Challenges and solutions to acquiring language and academic literacy for adolescent English language learners. A report to Carnegie Corporation of New York.* Washington, DC: Alliance for Excellent Education.

Stinnett, N., & DeFrain, J. (1985). *Secrets of strong families.* Boston: Little, Brown.

Suárez-Orozco, C., Suárez-Orozco, M. M., & Todorova, I. (2008). *Learning a new land: Immigrant students in American society.* Cambridge, MA: Harvard University Press.

Teachers of English to Speakers of Other Languages (TESOL). (2006). *PreK–12 English language proficiency standards: Augmentation of the world-class instructional design and assessment (WIDA) consortium English language proficiency standards.* Alexandria, VA: Author.

Thomas, W. P., & Collier, V. (1997). *School effectiveness for language minority students* (NCBE Resource Collection Series, No. 9). Washington, DC: National Clearinghouse for Bilingual Education.

Townsend, D., & Collins, P. (2008). English or Spanish? Assessing Latino/a children in the home and school languages for risk of reading disabilities. *Topics in Language Disorders, 28*(1), 61–83.

U.S. Department of Education, National Center for Education Statistics. (2010). *Teacher attrition and mobility: Results from the 2008–09 teacher follow-up survey* (NCES 2010–353). Accessed at http://nces.ed.gov/pubs52010/2010353.pdf on August 22, 2011.

U.S. Department of Health, Education, and Welfare. (1970). *HEW memorandum to school districts with more than five percent national origin-minority children.* Accessed at www2.ed.gov/about/offices /list/ocr/ell/may25.html on August 22, 2011.

Valdés, G. (1996). *Con respeto: Bridging the distances between culturally diverse families and schools: An ethnographic portrait.* New York: Teachers College Press.

Vaughn, S., & Linan-Thompson, S. (2003). Group size and time allotted to intervention: Effects for students with reading difficulties. In B. R. Foorman (Ed.), *Preventing and remediating reading difficulties: Bringing science to scale* (pp. 299–324). Baltimore: York Press.

Wanzek, J., & Vaughn, S. (2010). Tier 3 interventions for students with significant reading problems. *Theory Into Practice, 49*(4), 305–314.

Wick, W. (1997). *A drop of water: A book of science and wonder.* New York: Scholastic.

INDEX

total physical response (TPR), 21

transitional/early-exit bilingual program, 28, 29

Vaughn, S., 50, 51

vocabulary

as a language objective, 12, 13

used in assessments, 37–38

Wanzek, J., 51

W-APT (WIDA-ACCESS Placement Test), 34

What Works Clearinghouse, 52

World-Class Instructional Design and Assessment (WIDA), 8, 32

Solution Tree

Solution Tree's mission is to advance the work of our authors. By working with the best researchers and educators worldwide, we strive to be the premier provider of innovative publishing, in-demand events, and inspired professional development designed to transform education to ensure that all students learn.

The mission of the National Association of Elementary School Principals is to lead in the advocacy and support for elementary and middle level principals and other education leaders in their commitment for all children.

Common Language Assessment for English Learners
Margo Gottlieb

Learn how to plan, implement, and evaluate common language assessments for your English learners. With this step-by-step guide, teachers, school leaders, and administrators will find organizing principles, lead questions, and action steps all directing you toward collaborative assessment. Yield meaningful information for and about EL learning preferences, build student self-assessment, and inform your instructional decision making based on reliable results. **BKF352**

Effective Program Evaluation, Second Edition
Mardale Dunsworth and Dawn Billings

Educators are increasingly coming to realize the importance of making decisions based on reliable, accurate data. This short guide provides a blueprint for evaluating academic programs, practices, or strategies within a simple, effective framework. It includes a step-by-step walkthrough of the program evaluation cycle and an appendix that explains vital concepts and vocabulary in accessible language. **BKF461**

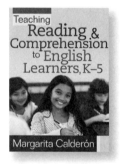

Implementing RTI With English Learners
Meg Ormiston

Learn why response to intervention is the ideal framework for supporting English learners. Find clear guidelines for distinguishing between lack of language proficiency and learning disability. Follow the application and effectiveness of RTI through the stories of four representative students of varying ages, nationalities, and language proficiency levels. Throughout the book, the authors illustrate the benefits of implementing RTI in a professional learning community. **BKF397**

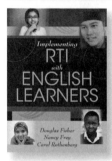

Teaching Reading & Comprehension to English Learners, K–5
Margarita Calderón

As more English learners enroll in school each year, teachers and administrators are concerned with the large gap in reading and academic standing between ELs and students performing at grade level. This book addresses the language, literacy, and content instructional needs of ELs and frames quality instruction within effective schooling structures and the implementation of RTI. **BKF402**

Mobile Learning Devices
Kipp D. Rogers

Do you share doubts with parents about the use of mobile learning devices (MLDs) in the classroom? Learn exactly what mobile learning is, how to introduce MLDs into your school, and how to ensure that teachers and students use them appropriately to enhance 21st century learning. Logistical implementation tips and examples of effective lesson plans are included. **BKF445**

Solution Tree | Press
a division of
Solution Tree

Visit solution-tree.com or call 800.733.6786 to order.